Zenaide Alexeievna Ragozin, Esaias Tegnér

Frithjof, the Viking of Norway, and Roland, the Paladin of France

Zenaide Alexeievna Ragozin, Esaias Tegnér

Frithjof, the Viking of Norway, and Roland, the Paladin of France

ISBN/EAN: 9783743337541

Manufactured in Europe, USA, Canada, Australia, Japa

Cover: Foto ©ninafisch / pixelio.de

Manufactured and distributed by brebook publishing software (www.brebook.com)

Zenaide Alexeievna Ragozin, Esaias Tegnér

Frithjof, the Viking of Norway, and Roland, the Paladin of France

By Zenaide A. Ragozin

The Story of Chaldea. 12°. Illus.	$1.50
Half leather, gilt top	1.75
The Story of Assyria. 12°. Illus.	1.50
Half leather, gilt top	1.75
The Story of Media, Babylon, and Persia. 12°. Illus.	1.50
Half leather, gilt top	1.75
The Story of Vedic India. 12°. Illus.	1.50
Half leather, gilt top	1.75

Siegfried and Beowulf. 12°. Illus. $1.50
Frithjof and Roland. 12°. Illus. 1.50

G. P. PUTNAM'S SONS, NEW YORK AND LONDON.

FRITHJOF'S FIRST BEAR.

Tales of the Heroic Ages

FRITHJOF
The Viking of Norway

AND

ROLAND
The Paladin of France

BY

ZENAÏDE A. RAGOZIN

Member of the Royal Asiatic Society of Great Britain and
Ireland; of the American Oriental Society, etc.
Author of "Chaldea," "Vedic India,"
"Siegfried and Beowulf," etc.

G. P. PUTNAM'S SONS
NEW YORK & LONDON
The Knickerbocker Press
1899

COPYRIGHT, 1899
BY
ZENAÏDE A. RAGOZIN
Entered at Stationers' Hall, London

The Knickerbocker Press, New York

CONTENTS

FRITHJOF

	PAGE
I.—Boy and Girl	3
II.—King Bele and Thorsten, Viking's Son	8
III.—Frithjof's Three Heirlooms	15
IV.—Frithjof's Wooing	27
V.—King Ring	33
VI.—Frithjof Plays Chess	39
VII.—In Balder's Grove	43
VIII.—Farewell	47
IX.—On the High Seas	63
X.—In Earl Angantyr's Hall	70
XI.—Frithjof's Return	79
XII.—Balder's Funeral Pyre	87
XIII.—Frithjof the Viking	92
XIV.—An Unbidden Guest	102
XV.—On the Ice	108
XVI.—The Temptation	111
XVII.—King Ring's Death	119
XVIII.—The Election	122
XIX.—The Vision	126
XX.—Reconciliation	131
Note on the 'Frithjof-Saga"	140

Contents

ROLAND

PART FIRST.—GANELON'S TREASON

	PAGE
I.—King Marsilius Holds a Council at Saragossa	147
II.—Charlemagne Holds a Council at Cordova,	152
III.—Ganelon's Embassy and Treason	165
IV.—The Rear-Guard—Roland's Doom	178

PART SECOND.—ROLAND'S DEATH

I.—Before the Battle	187
II.—The Battle	195
III.—The Olifant	209
IV.—Oliver's Death	216
V.—The Archbishop's Last Blessing	225
VI.—Roland's Death	230

PART THIRD.—RETRIBUTION

I.—First Reprisal—Charlemagne's Dreams	236
II.—Scenes at Saragossa	244
III.—The Obsequies	253
IV.—Roland Avenged	259
V.—The Traitor's Punishment	271
Note on the "Chanson de Roland"	283

ILLUSTRATIONS

	PAGE
FRITHJOF'S FIRST BEAR . . *Frontispiece*	
IN BALDER'S GROVE	44
INGEBORG'S WATCH BY THE SEA . . .	62
FRITHJOF IN SINGLE COMBAT . . .	72
QUEEN AND VIKING	106
OFF FOR THE CHASE!	112
FACSIMILE OF A PAGE OF THE "CHANSON DE ROLAND" (LAY OF ROLAND) . . From a MS. of the XIIth Century, now at Oxford in the Bodleian Library.	146
CHARLES RECEIVES THE ENVOYS OF THE HEATHEN KING MARSILIUS . . .	154
ARCHBISHOP TURPIN BLESSES THE FRENCH ARMY LEFT AT RONCEVAUX . . .	192
HAUBERKS, WORN OVER TUNICS, AND PENNANTS . . . . From Seals, XIIth Century.	206
STEEL HELMET WITH NOSE-GUARD (NASEL). From Seals, XIIth Century.	206

v

	PAGE
Roland's Death Blast on the Olifant .	212
Statues of Roland and Oliver in the Portals of the Cathedral at Verona, in Northern Italy	220
XIIth Century.	
Archbishop Turpin, Himself Dying, Blesses the Dead Peers Laid at his Feet by Roland. Roland Brings his Friend Oliver's Body .	228
Roland Trying to Break Durendal against a Rock; and Roland Blowing the Olifant .	232
From a Stained-Glass Window in the Cathedral at Chartres, France, XIIIth Century.	
The Archangel Gabriel Blesses the Dying Roland .	234
From a German MS., XIIth Century.	
Charles Views the Dead at Roncevaux, Seeking for his Nephew Roland. (In the Foreground, Archbishop Turpin and the Dead Peers) .	236
Charles Mourns over Roland's Body .	256
The Oriflamme .	260
After Mosaics in the Basilica of St. John Lateran in Rome, IXth Century.	
An Olifant	260
XIIth Century.	

Illustrations vii

	PAGE
DEMOISELLE AUDE KILLED BY THE TIDINGS OF ROLAND'S DEATH	272
JUGGLER (JONGLEUR)	290

From a MS. in the National Library in Paris, XIth Century.

FRITHJOF
THE VIKING OF NORWAY

I

BOY AND GIRL

OLD HILDING, King Bele's tried and trusted counsellor, resided at his handsome homestead with its rich and well-kept farm. Here the aged sage gladdened the restful idleness of his waning years watching the growth of two tender plants entrusted to his care—fairer the North had never seen: the one a lordly oak, straight of trunk, stately of crown, strong to defy the storm; the other a lovely rose scarce open, half dreaming in the bud. Frithjof was the youthful oak; but the rose was known to the sons of the North as Ingeborg the Fair. Not often was one seen without the other.

A proud lad was Frithjof the day that

he learned to read his first rune, for did he not hasten to teach it forthwith to willing Ingeborg? What boy happier than he when he took her in his light skiff out on the blue waters, and she clapped her little hands in the blitheness of her heart as he set the snowy sail? No nest too high for him to fetch down for her—the kingly eagle himself would hardly keep from him his eggs and young. No brook so wide and angry that he does not carry Ingeborg across, so her little white arm nestles at his neck. The first blossom which rewards his gardening, the first strawberry he espies in the woods, the first golden ear that ripens—he carries them all to his little queen.

But childhood's days are brief and fleet, and ere the elders look for the change, behold! the lad stands before them a well-grown youth.

And now young Frithjof began to go out a-hunting, but not as others go. Indeed not many would have cared to face their first bear unarmed, as he did, trusting not in sword or spear, but only in his own mighty sinews and dauntless spirit. Breast to breast he wrestled with the beast, and choked the breath out of him, safe himself, though not quite scatheless; and forthwith, unheeding the bleeding scratches, he loaded the shaggy monster on his shoulders and took it home straightway, where he laid it, triumphant, at Ingeborg's feet — his manhood's first achievement.

Then winter came, with the long home evenings, when all the housemates sat at ease, talking or resting, around the hearth, — perchance listening to young Frithjof, as, by the light of the great logs blazing in the vast fireplace, he read aloud ancient lays of Odin the All-Father's heavenly halls, where gods and goddesses disport themselves, ever youthful, fair, and vigorous. And there was not a goddess with whom Frithjof did not, as he read, secretly compare his own sweet playmate, with her hair falling in golden ringlets, her tender eyes, blue as the sky in spring, her delicate snow-white skin. But of all those old stories none moved him as that which tells how young Balder, the darling of the gods, done to death through the malice of one of them, is mourned by his faithful wife Nanna. He thought how gladly he would die, how gladly reside in the dark realm of Hel, the cruel queen of the dead, to be mourned as lovingly by one true maiden's heart.

Ingeborg meanwhile, King Bele's blooming daughter, sat at her loom day by day, singing the deeds of heroes at her work, as she wove them into the cunning tapestry, wherein, as she deftly handled the wool of many dyes, woods and cornfields started into life, and amidst them knights and foot-soldiers, in silver mail, with golden shields and lifted lances, waging fierce battles. And day by day the hero grew more like Frithjof in features and in bearing. She marked the likeness and took the greater pleasure in her work. And she would have begged of Mother Earth her fairest flowers, to wind them into wreaths for Frithjof's locks, and would have taken down the sun from the heavens to give it him for his shield; while he would have robbed the sea of its choicest pearls to grace Ingeborg's slender neck, and would have woven the pale moonbeams into a garment for her.

Old Hilding saw—and his heart misgave him. For the maiden was of royal blood, King Bele's only daughter, while Frithjof came of humble bonder[1] stock—even though his father, Thorsten, once King Bele's trusty squire, was now by him loved and honoured as his nearest comrade and friend.

"Beware, my son," the old man said to his ward; "let not this love of thine master thee; no good can come of it. Only where like mates with like are happiness and peace."

But Frithjof laughed the warning to scorn:

"The free-born man is second to no one. The world is the freeman's. What chance divided, chance may bring together. A mighty wooer is the sword. For her I will do battle with Thor himself, the fierce Thunderer. Bloom on, my white lily, and fear not: woe to them that would part us."

[1] *Bonder*—Scandinavian for "yeoman" or "farmer."

II

KING BELE AND THORSTEN, VIKING'S SON

IN his royal hall, leaning upon his sword, stands King Bele, and by his side stands Thorsten, the doughty bonder, the King's old brother-in-arms. Nigh on a hundred winters have passed over the two warriors' heads, and silvered their hair, and marked and lined their faces, till they look like ancient rocks, thickly covered with deeply graven runes. Such, in places, between mountains, stand old temples, relics of heathen ages, shrines of forgotten gods, half tottering to the ground,—yet much wise lore speaks from the walls, and many paintings tell of old heroic times.

"Our day is done," says Bele, "and night is coming on apace. The strongest mead tastes flat to me, and heavy feels the helmet to my brow. For earthly sights my eyes grow dim; but ever nearer shines Valhalla's light. My time is brief. Therefore, my friend, I have sent for our sons, my two and thy one. They should be firmly knit in love, as thou and I have been. And some warning words I fain would speak to the young eagles ere I go: not many more will they hear from these old lips."

Even as he spoke, the youths came in: Helge, the eldest, first, with gloomy brow and sullen eye. He was mostly found with priests and seers, by the great altar-stone; and even now, as he approached his father, his hands were bloody from the sacrifice. He was followed by the lad Halfdan, with sunny locks, of noble countenance, but too soft: it almost seemed as though he wore the sword for play—a maid in warrior's guise. Frithjof came last, by a head the tallest of the three, and stood between the King's sons as the full noon between dawn and dusk.

"Sons," spoke the King, "my day is

sinking low, and yours will soon be breaking. As ye are brothers, so be friends, and rule the land in harmony. Let Power stand guard at the borders, but Peace hold gentle sway within, in your safe keeping. Your swords should not threaten, but protect; your shields should be the padlocks on the peasant's barn. For kings can do nothing without the people, as the tree's leafy crown soon withers if its roots plunge into barren soil, which yields the sap but grudgingly to the trunk. Be never hard, King Helge,—only firm. Remember that the best-tempered steel bends most easily. Graciousness becomes a king as flower-wreaths a shield; and spring's mild breath opens the earth which wintry frost but hardens. A friendless man, however strong, dies as the lonely tree bereft of its bark. But in the midst of friends thou art safe as the forest tree, sheltered from storms, whose roots drink from the living brook. Thou, Halfdan, be mindful that cheerfulness graces the wise man, but that frivolity ill beseems a king. Honey alone makes not the mead

—it needs the bitter hops; a sword should be of steel, and a king should be half earnest even in his play. And, Halfdan, the way to a comrade, a faithful friend, is short, however distant his home; but it is long to a foe's house, even though it lay close by the road. Do not place confidence in everyone, unthinkingly. Choose one to trust, and look not for another; for what is known to three will soon be known to all."

Here Thorsten rose; he too had weighty words to speak:

"It is not meet, O King, that thou shouldst go to Odin all alone. We shared alike the changeful gifts of life; methinks the death-lot should be ours in common too. Son Frithjof, mark me; for age has whispered many a thing into my ear. Odin's birds dwell on graves in the far North, and they bring words of wisdom to the lips of the dying. Honour the gods, who send us pain and joy, as sunshine and storm, from heaven, who see into the heart's most secret chamber, be it never so closely locked. Obey the

King,—one hand should wield the royal power. Envy not him whose place is above thine: the sword needs must have a hilt as well as a blade. Great bodily might is a gift of the gods; but, Frithjof, the gift is worthless unless joined with wit: the bear, with the strength of twelve men, must yield to one. The day, my son, should not be praised before the evening, nor mead before 't is drunk, nor men's advice before the event has proved it good. So friends are proven true in need, and steel in battle. Therefore put not thy trust in ice of one night's freezing, nor in spring snow, not in the sleep of snakes, nor in woman's uncertain mind. Thyself must surely die and all that's thine must pass away; but one thing must as certainly endure: it is the name that thou wilt leave behind; so, Frithjof, turn thee from evil, bend thy will to what is good and noble, and do right. Thus wilt thou not have lived in vain."

Many more were the loving words spoken by the old warriors on that day. They told the youths of their long friendship, famous in the Northern lands, and how, through joy and sorrow, peace and strife, they had stood together, hand in hand, united until death. The King spoke much of Frithjof's valour and heroic might—gifts to be prized above royal blood; and Thorsten said much in praise of the crown and the glory of Norseland's kings. And both bequeathed their friendship to their sons as a treasure of great price.

"If you three keep together through life as ye stand here before me," King Bele said, "the man does not live in the North who can prevail against you. And now," he added, "take my greeting to my daughter, my red rose. She has grown up in rural retirement—such was my will. Shelter her still, that the rude storm-winds may not pluck or break the tender flower. To thee, O Helge, as to a father, I commit the care of her—as a daughter love her, my Ingeborg! But remember that sternness angers a noble heart, and that gentleness alone leads it, be it man's or woman's, to honour and right doing. When we are gone, lay us in two mounds, which ye shall raise one on each side of the blue bay; its waves shall sing our dirge. And, Thorsten, when the pale moon pours on the mountains her silver sheen, and the midnight dew lies cool upon the fields, thou and I, old friend, will still commune together as of old, from hill to hill, upon the happenings of the day. And now, sons, fare ye well! Go back to your work and play. For us, our way lies to All-Father's halls,—the place of rest, for which we long as long the weary rivers for the sea. Go, and the grace of Frey, and Thor, and Odin go with you!"

III

FRITHJOF'S THREE HEIRLOOMS

BELE and Thorsten, the two friends, had been laid in the mounds on each side of the bay, as they had ordered. Helge and Halfdan were elected joint kings by the people at a general meeting. Frithjof, being an only son, had no one with whom to share his inheritance and at once entered the homestead at Framnäs as master.

Truly, a fair inheritance: hills and valleys and woods, three miles each way, with the sea as boundary on one side. The heights were crowned with birchwood, and where they gently sloped, the golden barley ripened in the sun, and rye so tall a man might hide in it. Lakes not a few mirrored the mountains and the forests where antlered elks stalked majestic and drank from a hundred streams. And in the valleys the sheltered pastures were gay with herds of kine, sleek and heavy-uddered, and dotted with sheep, white and fleecy as the cloudlets which the spring breeze drives across the sky. And in the stables there stood, in stately rows, twice twelve fiery steeds, winds in harness, their manes braided with red ribbons, their hoofs glistening with polished shoes.

But the wonder of the place was the banquet-hall, a palace in itself, solidly built of fir trunks, well fitted. Six hundred guests hardly filled it at the great Yuletide feast. The board, of oak, stretched the whole length of the hall, waxed to a polish as bright as steel. The dais at the host's end was adorned with two statues of gods carved out of elmwood: Odin, with royal mien, and Frey, with the sun on his brow. Between the two was the host's seat, covered with a huge bearskin, black, with scarlet mouth and silver-mounted claws. It seemed but yesterday that Thorsten sat there, gravely yet genially entertaining his friends with many a wondrous tale of foreign lands, of vikings' ventures on the seas. Deep into the night they would sit, listening entranced, while the great logs blazed high in the deep stone hearth in the middle of the hall, and the stars peered down through the wide smoke-escape in the roof, and the fire-light played, gleaming and glinting, on the armours which hung all round the walls, with a sword between each two, flashing every now and then, like a shooting star on a winter night.

Great wealth was stowed away in the dwelling-house; cellars and garrets, closets and storerooms overflowed with substance. Nor was there lack of precious things taken in war or given in gracious token of friendship. Of these family treasures three were prized above all other possessions by Thorsten, and now by his son.

The first and most peerless was the sword Angurwadel, own brother to the lightning. It had been forged and tempered by wizard dwarfs, so went the story, and first worn by the hero Björn Bluetooth; but he soon lost both sword and life in single combat against bold Wifell, whose son was Viking, Thorsten's father. When Viking was a youth of fifteen winters, he and Angurwadel did battle with a savage Troll and slew him. The giant appeared in the land of a feeble and aged king, demanding his crown and only child, a lovely daughter of tender years, unless a champion were found who could fight and overcome him. There was no such champion among the old king's men, and the poor maid would surely have been carried away into the black forest, of which no man had ever seen more than the outside belt of trees, but for the youth and his magic sword. With one stroke Angurwadel cut in two the bellowing Troll, and rescued the maid. Now Frithjof owned it. When he drew it, a glory filled the hall like the brilliancy of the Northern light. The hilt was of gold and the blue steel of the blade was graven with countless runes, which showed dull in times of peace; but in battle, or when the owner's heart was moved in anger, they burned and glowed in ruby red, and woe to them that came across the blazing blade 'midst the blackness of the fray!—Great was the fame of that sword; it was known far and wide as the best in all the North.

Second in value of the three heirlooms was a massive ring of purest gold, a piece of matchless art, the work of Lame Waulund, the divine smith of the North. Thick it was, and broad and heavy, such as might fitly encircle a hero's arm. And on it the heavens were imaged, with the twelve immortal mansions where, month after month, the sun rests in his course, and Alfheim, Frey's own House of Light, whence the young sun each Yuletide begins again his long climb up to the topmost heaven. There, too, in the hall of the gods where Odin drinks mead in a golden cup, Balder sat upon his throne —the Midnight Sun; Balder the good, the blameless; then Balder dead, upon the funeral pyre, and, further still, in the realm of grewsome Hela, the pitiless ruler of the dead. These and many more scenes, all telling of the struggle between light and darkness in the heavens above, and below, in the human breast, were portrayed on the ring. In the clasp was set a ruby of enormous size. Through a long line of ancestors on the mother's side the ring had come down to Thorsten.

Once it was lost—stolen by a pirate of whom nothing was known but that he called himself Sote and roamed the Northern seas. Then there came a rumour that Sote had landed on a remote shore and had gone, alive, into a huge grave-mound, into the vast chamber of which, lined with well cemented slabs, he had taken his ship and all his treasures; but that he had not found rest, and ghostly doings made the mound a terror for miles around. Thorsten heard the story. He and Bele forthwith mounted their dragon-ship, sped over the waves, and quickly reached the unknown strand. There before them rose the mound, looking as would a gigantic temple if it were domed with sward. Gleams of light weirdly shot out of it, and when the two comrades cautiously peered in through some chinks in the massive iron door, they beheld within the pirate's ship, serpent-shaped, pitch-black, all equipped with mast and rudder, and high up in the rigging there sat a frightful form, in a fiery mantle, with ireful eyes, rubbing away at a blood-stained sword-blade; but the stains would not go. And all around him, in the chamber, lay the gold-plunder, scattered and in heaps; the ring was on his arm. "Shall we go in," whispered Bele, " and fight the horror ? Two men against a fire-goblin ?" " One against one is champions' law," retorted Thorsten almost angrily; " I will dare the test alone." Bele would not hear of it, and they wrangled long and eagerly for the dangerous honour, till at last they agreed to cast lots in Bele's steel helmet; they shook it, and when one lot was taken out, Thorsten knew it for his own in the pale starlight. He struck the door with his lance, and so powerful was that first shock that bolt and lock gave way; the door flew open, and he descended many steps. . . . When people asked him in later years what he had seen that night, he would shudder and keep silence. But Bele, who listened anxiously outside, told how he had first heard what seemed like a song of the evil Trolls,—then a clanging, as of swords at deadly play,—then fearful shrieks,—then sudden stillness. And Thorsten rushed out, pale, dazed, half witted—for it was Black Surtur, Death's own self, with whom he had wrestled. But the ring was on his arm. And in after times, whenever he showed it, he would say :—" This ring has cost me dear : once in my life I quaked with fear—that was when it was lost and I won it back."—Great was the fame of that ring ; it was known far and wide as the finest in all the North.

The third family heirloom was the ship Ellide. A strange tale was told of how she came into the possession of Viking, old Thorsten's father. One day, returning home from a long voyage, he was sailing along the coast, when he saw a dismasted wreck swaying on the gently heaving waters, and on it sat a man, who seemed to enjoy the play of the sunlit waves. He was tall of stature and of lofty mien, with a countenance open and cheery, yet changeful as the sea itself. He was clad in a long blue mantle, his belt was of gold, studded with red corals; his beard was white as the sea-foam; his locks were of a dark sea-green. Viking steered for the wreck, took off the man, who seemed all drenched and chilled, and cared for him at his own home, with food and drink, by his own reviving hearth-fire. The stranger accepted the care, well pleased; but when his host would have urged him to rest in his own warm bed, he laughed, and said: "The wind is good enough for me, nor is my ship as bad as thou mayest think: between now and night it will, I trow, carry me a good hundred miles. Have hearty thanks for thy kindly urging. Fain would I leave thee a gift to remember me by; but my substance all lies in the deep. Still, if to-morrow thou shouldst happen to walk the way of the beach, and thou shouldst take a look around, thou mayest perchance find something." Next day Viking stood on the beach, when lo!

swift as the sea-eagle in pursuit of its quarry, a dragon-ship flew into the river's mouth. No sailor was to be seen, not even a steersman. Yet she threaded her way in and out between the cliffs and banks, as though instinct with mind. As she neared the strand, the sails reefed themselves; the anchor dropped and bit the sand. Viking stood gazing in speechless wonder; but in the whisper of the playful waves he plainly heard a voice:—
"God Ægir, ruler of the seas, was thy guest yesterday. Mindful of his debt of kindness, he sends thee the dragon—take his gift."

And a right royal gift was the ship. In her shapely sides the oaken timbers were not joined, as usual, by practised carpenter's hand, but grown together as in a living body. Long-stretched as a sea-serpent, the neck rose in bold yet graceful curves, carrying high the head with red mouth wide open; the sides were blue, gold-spotted; at the stern the mighty tail uncoiled in rings, silver-scaled; the wings were black, tipped with scarlet, and when she unfurled them she could keep pace with the storm-wind and far exceed in fleetness the eagle's flight. When filled with men in armour, she seemed like a royal city or a swimming castle.—Great was the fame of that ship; it was known far and wide as peerless in the North.

These and many other beautiful things did Frithjof inherit from his father. A wealthier heir could hardly have been found in the Northern lands, unless it were among the sons of kings. And truly, if not of royal blood, he was of royal soul —gentle, and generous, and of lofty mind, and his fame grew with each day. Among his men there were twelve grey-haired warriors, Thorsten's own comrades, princes among men, although of simple birth, like himself, with breasts like steel corslets, and broad brows all scar-lined. And in their midst, upon the bench of honour, there sat a youth—a rose in a wreath of withered leaves. Björn was his name. With a child's joyousness he had a man's firmness and an old man's wisdom. He had grown up with Frithjof, and the two were sworn brothers: they had mixed blood and drunk it, after the ancient custom, held sacred by the sons of the North, and exchanged an oath—to share good and evil fortune through life and to avenge each other in death.

Now, at the funeral feast, Frithjof sat, a tearful host, on his father's seat, henceforth his own, between Odin and Frey, listening to praises of the dead, from the lips of friends and guests, and in the song of heaven-taught Skalds. For such, of old, was the custom in the North.

IV

FRITHJOF'S WOOING

THE earth has donned once more her robe of green; few dragon-ships still loiter along the strand, and those but wait for their youthful crews to take them out, on foreign ventures bound, as is Norsemen's wont. But Frithjof's thoughts do not roam the seas; he seeks the solitude of the woods, these moonlit nights of lovely May.

A few short days ago he was the proudest, the happiest of men: he had bidden the young Kings to be his guests at Framnäs, and Ingeborg had come with them. The two had sat together, hand in hand, and their talk had been of their common childhood, when each day glistened with the morning dew of life. They had wandered together over rich meadows and in shady groves, and she had uttered many a little cry of joy as she found her own name cut in the silvery bark of the handsomest birches. But it was with a sigh that she confessed to her friend:

"How much better I feel here than in the royal castle! For Halfdan is boyish and Helge is harsh. One wants coaxing and the other obedience. And there is no one" (here she blushed like a wild rose)—"no one to whom I could confide a trouble, a sad thought. How different it was in our dear old Hildingsdale! The doves which we did raise together have been scared away by the hawks. Only one pair is left: take thou one, and I will cherish the other. If thou tie a message under its wing and let it go, it will straightway seek its mate."

As the spring whispers in the green lindens, so they whispered to each other all day long; they were whispering still when the sun went down.

Now she was gone, and all Frithjof's joyousness had gone with her. In a day or two he wrote a loving message and sent off the dove with it, but received no answer, for the bird would not leave its mate again.

This state of things was not at all to Björn's liking, and he wondered to himself: "What can have made our young eagle so still and moody? What shot has pierced his breast or lamed his wing? Surely there is no lack here of meat or honeyed mead, and there are Skalds enough, in faith, for them that love their never-ending songs. What can he be pining for?"

The steeds stamp the stable floor with impatient hoof, the falcons wildly shriek for quarry; Ellide sways restlessly in the harbour, tugging at her anchor: Frithjof heeds them not, but still, day after day, broods in silence and alone.

At last, one morning, he loosed the dragon-ship's bonds—she bounded from her moorings, and, steered by his will, bore him straight, with swelling sails, across the bay, to where the Kings sat on Bele's grave-mound, holding open court of justice. Proudly, yet respectfully, Frithjof stood before them, and spoke, without delay or preamble, what was in his heart:

"Fair Ingeborg, ye Kings, I love as my own soul, and crave her at your hands for my dear bride. Such surely was King Bele's intent, for it was by his will we grew up together in Hilding's keeping. True, my father was neither king nor earl, yet his name will live in song for many a year; the story of our race is told in runes on many honoured graves. I could easily win me a kingdom, but I would liefer stay at home and take care of your kingdom for you—guarding your royal castle and the poor man's hut alike. We are here on Bele's mound—he hears me as I sue to you; hear ye, his sons, his voice as he speaks to you from the grave!"

Then King Helge started angrily to his feet, and spoke in scornful tones:

"Our sister is not for the bonder's son. The daughter of the gods must wed with royal blood. Though thou shouldst, by force of arms, compel men to hail thee greatest of Norseland's sons, never shall maid of Odin's blood mate with a low-born adventurer. Nor is there any call for thee to take thought for my realm; I can hold it and care for it myself. But I would fain have thee my retainer: there is a place free among my men-at-arms—thou art welcome to it."

"Man of thine I will never call myself," Frithjof answered quick, in clarion tones; "I will be my own man, as my father was before me. Stand by me, Angurwadel! Too long hast thou been idle!"

And as he spoke, the blue lightning of the steel flashed forth from the silver scabbard; the runes upon the blade burned in angry red.

"Thou black-hearted King!" quoth Frithjof sternly, "were this spot not hallowed by the peace of a beloved grave, my trusty sword should teach thee a lesson. As it is, thou hadst best heed my warning: see thou comest not too near its range!"

And turning to where King Helge's golden shield hung on a limb of the oak beneath which he sat, Frithjof with one mighty stroke cleft it in twain: the halves fell to the ground with loud clang, and the hollow mound echoed the ominous sound.

"Well done, friend Angurwadel!" cried the youth. "Now lie still and dream of nobler deeds; thy blazing runes extinguish for a while. Home now, across the blue waters—home!"

V

KING RING

THE feast was ended. King Ring pushed back his carved gilt chair. Warriors and Skalds arose, to hear their liege's words; for his wisdom and piety were famed in all the lands of the North. His own land was as a pleasure-ground of the gods. Never did those verdant valleys, those shady woods, resound with the evil noises of war. Peacefully the crops ripened there, and the roses bloomed. Justice sat enthroned, severe yet gracious, on the granite judgment-seat. Peace alone paid the State's yearly dues, in golden grain, heaped high on the ground, more precious far than coined ore. Black-breasted ships sailed the waters with white pinions, sent from a hundred lands, freighted with riches for the rich. And freedom dwelt with peace in happy harmony. Loved as a father, the old King ruled; yet the people's voice was raised without fear or restraint at the Ting-meetings,[1] and every man was free to speak his mind there. Thus for thirty years peace and prosperity had dwelt together under such gentle rule.

And now, when King Ring pushed back his carved gilt chair from the banquet-table, all rose expectant, to hear the words that would fall from his honoured lips. But he sighed, and his speech was sad:

"On purple couch my queen reclines in Freya's happy bowers above—Freya, the goddess of love and beauty; but here below the grass is green upon her grave, and flowers' perfume lingers around her mound. Never may I find another wife so sweet, so fair, a mate so queenly on the throne. She has found her guerdon in Valhalla,

---

[1] *Ting*, Anglo-Saxon *Thing*—general meeting of the people, to discuss important questions. From the Ting's decision there was no appeal.

but vainly land and children call for their gracious queen and mother. King Bele has many a time been our guest, here in this very hall. He left a daughter. Her have I chosen in my mind. True, she is but young, just budding into bloom, playmate of lilies and of roses, while many a winter's snow lies on my scanty locks. Still, should she find in her heart some love to give an honest man, even though age have already marked his brow, and womanly care for tender motherless babes, then fain would my winter share with her spring this throne. Go then, my trusty ones, to her, with gold and bridal gear from the old oaken safe, and ye, Skalds, follow with song and harp, for festive strains should brighten the solemn royal wooing."

As the King ordered, so was it done. Warriors and Skalds, with attendants many and well equipped, a long procession, bearing gifts and honourable offers, set forth to seek King Bele's sons.

And right royally they were received—entertained in state for three whole days.

But on the fourth morning they asked what answer they should take home, as they might not tarry longer.

Then King Helge summoned the high-priest and his assistants, that they might, with all due ceremonies and sacrifices, inquire into the will of the gods in a matter of so much import to Bele's royal house. The sacred falcon was brought forth, the steed was led into the grove where stood the sacrificial altar-stone, in the mysterious dusk of overarching murmuring boughs, and the sacred acts were performed amid a deep, awed silence, broken only by the chanted prayers or muttered words of meaning known only to the priests. At last the divine verdict was proclaimed: fear and dismay fell on those that heard. The falcon's flight was low and timid and in the wrong direction. The victim's heart and lungs were unhealthy and ill-placed. Indeed, so disastrous were the signs that King Helge, terrified and trembling, rejected King Ring's wooing on the spot, and bade his messengers depart without delay.

King Halfdan, always light-hearted, laughed loud and thoughtlessly.

"Farewell, ye feasts and festivals!" he cried. "Oh, were King Greybeard but here himself! Right lustily would I help his old limbs into the saddle!"

The envoys departed, bitterly angered. They told their story to King Ring, sparing no detail of their insulting dismissal. He said little, but his words were grim:

"King Greybeard will yet show the youngsters that he is not too old to avenge his honour."

He struck with his spear the iron shield—the clang of which summons the people to arms, high and low—where it hung in the open field on the boughs of an ancient linden tree. The dragon-ships came crowding in, with blood-red crests; the helmets nodded in the breeze. War-heralds hurried right and left.

King Helge heard, and was greatly perturbed in mind; for, though arrogant and hard of heart, he was not brave. He knew that King Ring was very powerful, and, though he loved not war, would, if he once took the field, be a most dangerous foe, for he was wise and skilled in the deadly game, and his people loved him and would follow him to the world's end, and fight for him unto death. Knowing, too, that their first object would be to carry away Ingeborg, he ordered her to retire into the enclosure of Balder's temple, thus placing her in the pure and gentle keeping of the best-loved among the gods. Not that the place offered safety from attack,—the enclosure was but wood, and not otherwise fortified. But it was, to all the Norse people, the most sacred of all sanctuaries, and a woman or maid who had taken refuge there was secure from the approach of man: pain of death stood on the violation of this sanctuary.

There loving Ingeborg sat day after day, sad and fearful of what the next might bring. And as she bent over her embroidery frame, plying her needle, sorting her silks and gold threads, many a tear fell on it or rolled unchecked upon her bosom: not purer the morning dew on the lily of the valley!

VI

FRITHJOF PLAYS CHESS

FRITHJOF, meanwhile, had not yet made up his mind to go to sea like his comrades, and leave his love to Helge's untender care. He lived on, moody and moping, in the seclusion of his freehold of Framnäs; and his faithful Björn, though chafing and puzzled at the unwonted idleness, stayed loyally with him. They found little matter for converse, and spent much of the slow-dragging time at the chessboard. One day, as they were fighting a particularly hard battle with the gold and silver men and pawns, old Hilding, Frithjof's foster-father, entered with ill-boding, clouded brow. Frithjof welcomed him most cordially:

"Sit here by me on the bench. Rest

thee and ply the drinking-horn, while I give my mind to these few last moves, which must lead me to certain victory."

But Hilding had that to say which brooked not trifling or delay.

"Frithjof," he began, "Bele's sons send me to thee, with words of peace. Let my voice lend weight to their suing. For I come, a messenger of evil, to tell thee that the country's only hope lies in thee."

"Björn," said Frithjof, intent on the game, as though he had not heard the old man's solemn pleading, "danger threatens thy king. A common pawn alone can save him, and if he fail him, then must the king fall—it is his fate."

"Frithjof," the old man began again, "listen, and mark my words: make not light of the eagles' power. Though they may quake before Ring's might, they are strong to harm the likes of thee."

"Björn, I see thou wouldst trap my bishop; but he can meet the shock: see—he retires into his stronghold, well protected."

The old man now shifted his ground:

"Ingeborg sits, a captive, in Balder's house, and weeps her days away. Cannot *she* lure thee into action with her blue eyes tear-dimmed and sad?"

"Björn, and wouldst thou hurt my queen? her I cherished from childhood's days? the best and dearest in the game? Whatever else betide, I am *her* champion ever."

"Frithjof! Frithjof!" the old man exclaimed angrily at last, "wilt thou not hearken? Shall thy foster-father hie him home unanswered, because, for sooth, a silly game will not be played to an end?"

Then the youth rose, and taking Hilding's hand, said gravely:

"Father, thou hast thine answer. Methinks I have made my meaning plain. Ride back to them that sent thee, and let them clearly understand: after the insults they have heaped on me, everything is at an end between us; I will not take up arms for them."

"Son," said Hilding sadly, "thou must e'en choose thine own way. Thy wrath is just—I cannot blame it. Yet I could wish thou mightst forego it. May Odin turn all things for the best!"

Thus spoke he—and was gone.

VII

IN BALDER'S GROVE

"LET Bele's sons send out the war-call from vale to vale! *I* go not to the field. In Balder's halls—*there* is my battle-field, *there* is my world!"

Such was the sum of Frithjof's broodings after Hilding's ill-omened visit. All his thoughts now centred on one fierce intent: he would see Ingeborg once more, would speak with her, assure himself that neither wile nor violence could take from him the love that was the sunshine of his soul. At peril of his life he would enter the sacred enclosure. He opened his heart to his blood-brother Björn, who little recked of law or danger, so he could serve his beloved Frithjof. They consulted together and decided to let Ellide take them some night to that part of the temple-grounds which, bordering on the sea, was easy of access, unguarded and unbarred. They managed to let Ingeborg know of their coming, so that she was watching for them, and met Frithjof a short distance from the place where they landed, as he made his way alone in the pale dusk of a Northern spring night. They bent their steps from the strand towards the temple, and Frithjof, feeling the maiden's slender frame tremble on his supporting arm, whispered to her words of courage and of cheer:

"Beloved, why quakest thou? Thou hast no cause for fear. Björn stands out there with bared sword and warriors enough to guard us, should need be, against a world. I myself would brave a world for thee, to hold thee thus. 'T were joy to be borne away to Valhalla's heights, wert but thou my Valkyrie[1]: to have thee bend over me as I lie on the bloody field,

---

[1] The Valkyries, in Norse mythology, were the heavenly maidens, daughters of Odin, who chose, by his command, the warriors who were to fall in battle, and carried them to Valhalla, the abode of the brave.

IN BALDER'S GROVE.

look in my face with thy dear eyes, then lift me on thy wind-winged steed; to soar with thee,—up, up, to Odin's heavenly halls,—what fate more blessed? What whisperest thou in such affright? Is it Balder's wrath thou dreadest? Why, he cannot be wroth with us. He too did love, the gentle god, was faithful unto death. Did he not love sweet Nanna, his wife, even as I love thee?"

As Frithjof spoke, they entered the temple. Even there the darkness was not so dense but that they could dimly perceive the god's carved image in its prominent position. He drew the timid maiden towards it.

"See!" he said; "he is near. How mildly he looks down on us! Come, bend thy knee. There is no sight in the wide world more pleasing in Balder's eyes than two hearts plighting their troth for life and death."

The prayer which Ingeborg offered from the depth of her pure heart, and the many soothing words uttered in her friend's familiar voice, partly banished the maiden's anxious fears. It did not seem natural to her to fear when he was with her. Nor could she feel that she was doing any wrong in conversing with him as she had done all her life unchidden. So the hours sped swiftly on in loving, innocent communing. Still she did not forget the danger which Frithjof was challenging by his daring deed, and it was she who noted the signs of coming day,—the lark's early song, the first rosy streak of dawn; but not before the sun had burst forth in unclouded splendour could Frithjof tear himself away. But not for long. Emboldened by the success of this first venture, he repeated it again and again, and these nightly meetings became the one joy of the two young creatures so wantonly parted by one man's wicked pride of rank.

VIII

FAREWELL

ONE night Ingeborg waited more anxiously than usual. She waited long. In the first hours her heart beat high with hope. As the night waxed older it sank lower and lower. The hours dragged more and more slowly, and hope all but died.

"Daybreak!" she thought, "and Frithjof cometh not. Ah me, but man is hard! For the sake of his pride—the thing he calls his honour!—he is ever ready, without a qualm, to crush a faithful heart. Poor woman clings to his breast as the humble lichen to the rock, with a hundred little tender rootlets, drawing its sustenance from the tears of night."

It had been Ting-day. The people

were to have met, presided over by the Kings, at Bele's grave. With many prayers and tears untold, and a thousand coaxing ways, Ingeborg had succeeded in winning Frithjof's promise that he would seek the Kings, there, in the presence of the dead and before the face of the living, to offer them his hand once more for old friendship's sake,—and he was to have come to her straight from the meeting. And now day was breaking, and he had not come! In her long night-vigil she had passed through all the stages from hopeful joyousness to despair. She had at last even come to acknowledge herself guilty in having defied the law of the sanctuary. And now the punishment was coming: she would lose Frithjof, would pay with a life's misery for a few hours of unthinking happiness. Yet her heart rebelled against the sentence. She had not intended, nor, she thought, done any wrong. Could Balder, the mild, the loving, frown so sternly on a maiden's innocent love? But, as the hours crept on, the last traces of youth's confidence and self-will fell from her, and, in the place of the thoughtlessly, harmlessly happy girl, there stood a woman, braced to suffer and endure, sternly resolved to meet her fate in solitude and seclusion as bravely as the hero meets his out in the turmoil of the world. She had but just schooled herself to this hardest of all lessons, when lo! Frithjof stood before her.

"At last!" she cried, rushing towards him. "So late! Still thou comest. Welcome!"

But a glance at his face made her recoil, terrified: she read nothing but evil on that gloomy brow. A moment's silence, to collect her strength; then she spoke:

"Frithjof! tell me all. The worst will scarcely be news to me; I have felt it coming all through this dreadful night, and am prepared."

Without a word of endearment or preamble, putting a strong curb on his passion of anger and sorrow, Frithjof began his tale:

"I came to the Ting. 'T was held on the mound, and from its foot up the sides, to the very top, shield to shield, hand on hilt, Norseland's freemen stood, in serried, orderly ranks. Upon the stone judgment-seat King Helge sat, dark as the thunder-cloud, and by him Halfdan, a grown-up boy, carelessly leaning on his sword. I stepped up and stood before them. I spoke:—'King Helge, War stands at the border and strikes the battle-shield. Thy realm is threatened. Give me thy sister, and my arm is thine, to fight thy battles loyally. Let all ill feeling be forgotten—I would not willingly be at feud with Ingeborg's brother. Cast prejudice away! With one word thou savest thy crown and thy sister's heart. Here is my hand: by Thor I swear, 't is offered for the last time in friendship.'—A murmur, as of stormy sea-waves, swept over the Ting; a thousand swords struck applause against a thousand shields. And voices rose here and there, and swelled into one mighty roar:—'O give him Ingeborg! His is the best sword in all our land. Give him Ingeborg!'—My dear old foster-father, Hilding with the silver beard, stood up and spoke words of great wisdom, weighty as a practised champion's sword. Even Halfdan rose from the royal seat and begged for us. In vain! The sun might as well expect to draw flowers from the naked rock as prayers to cause a human stirring in that stony breast or on that pallid phantom face. With cold contempt he spoke:—'The bonder's son might even yet call Ingeborg his bride. But the sacrilegious violator of the sanctuary would hardly, methinks, be a fit mate for the daughter of Valhalla. Speak, Frithjof: didst thou not break the peace of Balder's temple? Didst thou not see and speak with my sister there at night, when the day hid its light from your monstrous deed? Yes, or No? Speak!'—A shout went up from the ring of men:—'Say "No!" We will believe thy word and woo for thee! Thorsten's son is the equal of kings. Say "No," and Ingeborg is thine!'—'The weal or woe of my whole life hangs on a word,' I said; 'but let not that, O King, dismay thee: I would not buy Valhalla's joys by a lie, certainly not those of earth.

Thy sister and I did meet and speak at night in Balder's temple; but not for that did I break the peace of the holy place.' I had no more to say. A groan of horror ran through the Ting. Those nearest me recoiled and fled, as I had suddenly been pest-stricken. Wherever I turned, my glance met blanched cheeks, set lips, the stony stare of fear. Helge had won the day! In tones low and ominous as those of Vala, the dead seeress, when she prophesied to Odin the fate of the bright Asas[1] and dark Hela's victories, he spoke: 'Exile or death is what our fathers' law leaves me free to order for such a deed as thine. But I will be merciful, even as Balder is, whose sanctuary thou hast desecrated. Far out in the Western sea there lies a cluster of islands, over which Earl Angantyr holds sway. As long as Bele lived, the Earl sent yearly tribute as agreed between them, but not since Bele's death. Go—demand the tribute, and bring it home: thus mayest thou redeem thy forfeit life and honour.' And he added

---

[1] *Asas*—the "bright ones," the gods.

a mean, evil-minded taunt :—' Heavy of hand is Angantyr said to be, and to roll in gold, like Fafner, the dragon. But how should even a new Fafner stand against our young Sigurd ! To overcome him truly were a deed more worthy of a man than to talk a maiden's sense away. Next summer, then, we shall expect to see thee, with thine honour washed clean—and, what's more, with the gold. If not, thou art shamed forever before the world, and banished from the country for life.' This was the sentence ; and the meeting's end."

Ingeborg had listened with all her soul, without putting in a word. Now she merely asked :

"Thy resolve ? "

"Is any choice left me ? " he answered bitterly. "Is not my honour bound in this behest ? I must redeem it, though Angantyr did hide his miserable gold in the waters of Nastrand, the river of the dead. This very day I sail."

"And leavest me ? "

"Never ! We go together."

"Impossible ! "

"Listen; oh, listen first! Thy wise brother, in his malice, forgot that Angantyr was my father's friend as well as Bele's. He may give me the gold for the asking. If not, I have a friend of eloquence keener than mine—here at my left thigh. I then send the treasure home to Helge, and lift the curse forever from our names. But we ourselves—thou and I, my Ingeborg,—we bid Ellide take us into strange, far-distant seas, to milder climes. What is the North to me? Let the poor slave cling to the soil to which he is bound; I will be free to come and go, as my own mountains' wind. A little dust from my father's grave-mound and thine —that is all we care to take of our native land. And then—beloved! there is a warmer sun, a fairer sky, than these—a sky whose stars, divinely bright, look down on soft summer nights upon laurel groves where a happy pair may wander unchid. My father used to tell us, on long winter evenings, by the fitful blaze of the hearth, of the blue seas of Greece with their many isles, where once upon a time there lived a mighty people, whose gods dwelt in high marble temples. The people is gone, of the temples nought is left but here and there a slender column-shaft, around which are twined creepers of luxurious growth, such as the North has never bred. The earth itself is beautiful and bears a plenty of all that men may need to live and thrive; golden apples of wondrous richness glow amidst dark, shining foliage; purple grapes hang luscious on leafy vines. There, Ingeborg, we will make us a home, a little heaven of our own. Oh, happiness *can* be reached—it only needs the courage to grasp and hold it. Come! Haste! Each word that we still loiter to speak, but steals so much from our appointed count of happy days and hours. All is ready; Ellide impatiently spreads and strains her dark eagle pinions, eager for the distant flight, and favouring breezes blow straight from these shores, once friendly, but now how rude and unkind! But—how is this? Hast thou no word? So grave? So cold? Dost doubt me? hesitate? . . ."

Ingeborg had listened to Frithjof's glowing speech sad and unresponsive, although he, carried away by his own fancy, by the picture which stood before him more and more vivid as his own words conjured it, did not at first notice her attitude. Now, as he paused, dismayed at finding her so unmoved, she said, in a low, gentle voice, which struck a chill to his heart:

"I cannot go with thee."

"Not go with me?"

"Thou, Frithjof, in all this misery, art still fortunate: thou art a man, thine own master, free to steer thy ship at thine own will! 'T is not so with me. My fate is in the hands of others. To suffer, renounce, pine in silence—so live and so die—that is a woman's freedom, king's daughter though she be."

"Not so. Thy will can make thee free indeed. Does not thy father sleep in yonder mound?"

"Helge is my father now. Such was King Bele's will. Oh, believe me, this last night—this endless, dreadful night, when I watched for thee, and thou camest not—it has made many things clear to me. I have chosen—my place is here. I have done with childhood's dreams. . . . And yet, as I listened to thy poet's fancies, of blessed islands in a summer sea, methought the old familiar voices spoke to me again out of those same dreams. A moment's weakness! That too is done with. I stay. And then—what have I to seek in the South, child of the North that I am? I would sicken with longing for my own pale sun, and my gaze would hang forever on the Northern star, that sentinel set in the heavens to watch over our fathers' graves. And as for thee—a man! Why, the fair wilderness thou paintest would soon become the grave of thy manhood and all thy deeds to be. Thy shield would rust, and with it thy free spirit. No! that shall never be! *I* will not be the one to steal my Frithjof's name out of our people's songs, to be sung by Skalds as yet unborn. Be wise, my friend. Let us not idly strive against our fate. Out of our life's wreck let us at least save honour—for happiness is gone. We must part."

"Why must we? Because thou hadst a sleepless night?"

"Because my honour and thy worth demand it."

"Woman is honoured in the love of man."

"Man loves not longer than he can respect."

"Senseless whims do not command respect."

Frithjof was fast losing control of himself. His voice grew harsh, his words bitter and cutting. Disappointment and despair seemed to change the very nature of his love, and he would almost, at that moment, have carried Ingeborg away by force, in true Viking fashion. It was more in threatening than in beseeching tones that he at last said warningly:

"Bethink thee well! Is this to be thy last word?"

"I have thought of all. It is the last."

"So be it, then!" he cried in a rage. "Farewell, Helge's sister!"

And he turned to go. But Ingeborg clung to him:

"O Frithjof, Frithjof! Not thus! not thus we part! Hast thou no loving glance, no touch of gentle hand, for thy youth's, thy childhood's friend? Thinkest thou I stand on roses, and send my whole life's happiness from me with laughing lips? Wert thou not my heart's morning dream? Every joy in life, all that is great and noble, bore in my thoughts thy semblance and thy name. Now, as thou goest from me, leave me not an image blurred, obscured! Overwhelm not with thy harshness the sorrowful soul who gives up the dearest thing she holds, be it here or in Valhalla's halls! The sacrifice is hard enough, in sooth; surely, a word of comfort were not ill bestowed! Full well I know thou lovest me, and the thought of me will follow thee many a moon. But the wild sea-life, the clash of arms, must deaden grief in time, till even of the dearest memory is left only a wan and pallid shade, which now and then may flit before thee in the morning mist, or sit by thee at the board, as thou drainest the silver-mounted horn, to pledge thy comrades in the hour of victory. But I and my grief must abide together to the end. In widow's weeds, alone in my secret bower, my only pastime—when I am not looking out upon the sea where some venturesome keel, like thy own Ellide's, cuts its way through the foaming waves—to stitch broken lilies into my endless tapestry, until a spring, more merciful than others, takes the work out of my hands, and for each poor dead lily strews a live lily over my grave. Or, if I take up the harp, to throw all my long sorrow into song, my voice breaks, tear-choked, as now, and——"

"Enough! enough!" cried Frithjof, all his tenderness reawakened at sight of his dear playmate's anguish. "Thou hast conquered, Bele's daughter! Weep no more. Forgive my harshness—'t was but love disguised, to hide its hurt. It cannot wear the garb of anger long. Thou art my good spirit—let me learn from thee, my Vala with the rosy lips! I will bow me to necessity; I will go and leave thee;

but not hope—*that* I will take across the seas, and to the very gates of death. Hear, then, my vow: the first spring day shall see me back here. I will stand before Helge free from guilt, my task performed, my honour cleared, my pledge redeemed. Then will I demand thee, not of him—oh no! of Norseland's people, in open Ting; *that* is thy rightful guardian, thou daughter of a royal race! Who *then* gainsays me—let him beware!—Till then, farewell. Be true, forget not me; and as a pledge and token of our love, take this arm-ring, and wear it till I claim it again —and thee. See how the delicate white arm sets off great Waulund's work, with the heavenly signs so cunningly engraved on it! Farewell awhile, my love, my bride —oh, fare thee well! A few moons only —and the tide will turn."

He went. Ingeborg watched him long and wistfully, her own sad face untouched by the glow of hope which lit up his brow, but now so gloomy and despondent. Age seemed to have suddenly come upon her, with its sober views, its fears,—its power too, to face and bear the worst. The pain of a lifetime was in the smile with which she spoke, half unwittingly, words she would not have him hear—not yet!

"My noble Frithjof! Almost happy he goes, beguiled by his own daring into hope. The point of his good sword he would set against the breast of fate itself and cry, 'Avaunt!' Alas, poor Frithjof! Fate goes its way and laughs at Angurwadel. Thou little knowest that dark brother of mine even yet. 'T is not for a hero's open mind to fathom the depths of so evil a nature, a breast in which the fires of hate and envy burn unquenchable. He give thee his sister? Never! Rather his crown, his life! Me he would first sacrifice to Odin on the altar-stone—or else to Ring, the old man whom he has angered into war. . . . No! whatever way I look, I see no gleam of hope! But I am glad *he* thinks not so. Ye kind gods! oh, stand by him and leave me with my grief alone! In six moons, said he? Yes. He will come back, but not to Ingeborg!"

INGEBORG'S WATCH BY THE SEA.

IX

ON THE HIGH SEAS

INGEBORG was right when she said that a generous mind could never fathom the whole depth of a wicked one. Frithjof, as he busied himself with getting Ellide ready for the long and dangerous voyage, would have been amazed indeed could he have seen King Helge standing on a lonely spot of the wild shore, intent on mysterious incantations, for it was not generally known that he was a skilled wizard and had learned from the priests in whose society he spent most of his time not only how to worship the bright and beneficent powers,—the gods,—but also how to control the dark and evil ones. He was now holding converse with two mighty giants, Heid and Ham, the Trolls of the storm-wind and of the snow-storm, whom he had conjured into his presence and was instructing to wreck Ellide on the high sea, where none of her crew might escape.

No sooner had Ellide put out of the harbour and run out of sight of the shore than the Trolls began their work. Darkness as of descending night suddenly blackened the sky; waves, seething and heaving as from the lowest deep, lifted their crests of foam with thundering roar; the sea-gulls and other sea-birds flew shrieking and in wild haste they knew not whither. Lightning streaked the blackness with red flame, and the thunder rolled and rumbled continuously all around and overhead.

Frithjof knew the signs: a storm was brewing, such as is not often met even in those dangerous seas. But the prospect of a hard fight with the elements rather suited his present rebellious mood. Besides, he trusted in the powers of his magic ship, and looked forward to the conflict as to a more than usually exciting game, no more. So he rode out right into the midst of it, and would not even make for any of the islands where well-known harbours might have afforded him shelter.

"It was pleasanter, I admit," he said laughingly to Björn, "to sail across the mirror-like bay in the still moonlight and find Ingeborg waiting in Balder's grove. But a doughty Viking loves to share the wild winds' play. My Ingeborg would blush for her sea-eagle, should he fly landward, with drooping wing lamed by a breath of wind."

But the tempest grows fiercer with every minute; the sea seems to yawn down to its very bottom. The gale whistles viciously in the rigging, timbers crack ominously. Still Ellide does not quake, but bravely holds her course, leaping and plunging merrily along, like a frolicsome mountain goat. Now, however, the storm lashes itself into wilder fury still. A wintry chill spreads through the air, hail rattles against the shields hung along the sides of the ship, and snow quickly covers the deck. Seas mountain-high at the same time rush upon the doomed ship from both sides, and, as they clash and break, deluge and sweep her from poop to prow. She quivers as she emerges, half buried, from the grave which must reopen soon—and then even she, Ellide, though built by no human hands, must give up the fight.

Now, such a storm, with frost and driving snow, is unnatural in summer, and even unsuspecting Frithjof suddenly guessed the truth.

"Björn!" he shouted in a voice that was heard above the din and howl, "come, take the helm; hold it for thy life. A storm like this never came from Valhalla's powers. Witchcraft is at play. This is some of Helge's unholy work—some of his singing and conjuring. I will go up and look."

Nimble as the forest squirrel, he climbed to the top of the tallest mast and held a sharp lookout. And lo! he espied at no great distance what seemed a swimming islet, tossed loosely amidst the raging waves. Looking more intently he made out a huge whale, and on the creature's back the two Trolls, who were working hard, doing Helge's bidding: Heid in his snow-coat, looking like an ice-bear, and Ham in the shape of a storm-eagle, flapping a pair of gigantic wings.

"Now, Ellide, show thy mettle!" Frithjof cried excitedly. "Hear my voice, and if thou art indeed a daughter of the gods, if high courage doth dwell within thy oaken breast—on to them, Ellide, and let thy copper keel cut the whale in two!"

And Ellide hears her master's voice. She gives one mighty bound and angrily makes straight for the whale. A jet of steaming blood spurts high at the shock; the monster, hurt to death, sinks into the gaping chasm. At the same time two spears, hurled by an unfailing hand, pierce the ice-bear's and the eagle's breasts. And instantly the storm surceases, the heavens clear, the sun comes forth in splendour, as a king entering the audience-hall, and sheds the glory of his presence over ship and sea and land. Frithjof's joy was solemn and subdued.

"Ingeborg's prayers," he whispered, as his gaze rested on the smooth expanse and on the golden disk now sinking low behind some islands' verdant strand— "Ingeborg's prayers sped, pallid maidens, up to Odin's hall, and, bending lily-white knees on its golden floor, touched the divine revellers' hearts. To her be thanks!"

But Ellide has sorely felt the strain, and the shock with the whale has all but disabled her. Weary and bruised, she just creeps along. Still more weary are the men. So exhausted are they, that they hardly manage to stand, leaning on their swords, and when at last Ellide stops alongside one of the Orkney Isles, Björn and Frithjof almost carry them on land, and lay them in a circle around the fire which they have quickly lit. They are deeply mortified at their weakness, and the chiefs have to comfort them with cheering words:

"Be not ashamed, ye pale friends! Even Vikings are not always a match for the sea, and water-maidens' embraces are chilling and unmanning. But here comes the mead-horn on its welcome round. There's life and warmth in it. To it with a will! And health to Ingeborg!"

X

IN EARL ANGANTYR'S HALL

NOW, ye may like to hear how, in his hall strongly built of fir-trunks, with his men so grim and battle-tried, Earl Angantyr, Lord of the Orkneys, sat feasting on that day, and how, as the golden mead went round, they looked, in restful, pensive mood, out on the blue expanse, on which the sinking sun rested light, like to a golden swan.

In the bay of the broad window old Halwar stands on watch, one eye on the waves, the other on the mead. Silently he drains his horn and silently holds it out for more. Suddenly he throws it, empty, behind him on the floor, and cries:

"A ship, a ship! out there by the strand. But something is wrong with her.

In Earl Angantyr's Hall

Her crew seems in distress. Now they land, but queerly, i' faith: two giants are carrying the men to the land and lay them on the ground."

The Earl now joined old Halwar and took a look.

"Those are Ellide's wings," he said; "so Frithjof must be there. By his features, by his bearing, Thorsten's son is easily known—such a face is not often seen here in the North."

Here Viking Atle springs from the banquet-table, black-bearded, grim, his blood-shot eye alight with battle's fire.

"Now," he cries, "we shall see whether Frithjof can, as 't is said of him, cast a spell on steel, or whether he will sue for peace."

With him up spring twelve champions of the fiercest; waving their swords and maces they rush down to the beach, where tired Ellide lies, and Frithjof sits on the sand, speaking comforting words to his weary men.

"I could easily fell thee where thou sittest," Atle boastingly addressed him

by shocks less ponderous. The heavy drops stand on the wrestlers' brows, their breasts heave high and short, shrubs and stones fly all around. Their friends look on aghast and fearful of the end, yet in their hearts they praise alike each champion's bravery and skill. That fight was long remembered in all the Northern lands.

At last Frithjof felled his foe, and held him down with his knee.

"Had I but my sword," he cried, "thou black-bearded maniac, I should quickly make an end of thee."

"Have thy will," was Atle's proud retort. "Go, get thy sword; I have no wish to run away. We both must see Valhalla some day; I go now, thou mayest follow me to-morrow."

Frithjof seemed minded to take his prostrate foe's advice; already Angurwadel was raised above him, yet Atle did not stir. Such manliness touched the victor's generous heart; his anger fell, he cast the sword aside, and took the fallen man by the hand,

Then Halwar raised aloft his white staff.

"Enough!" he cried. "Your senseless brawl is pleasing to no one but yourselves. The meats have long stood steaming on the board, fish and fowls are growing cold, and I am sheer dying with thirst."

And so the two, now friends, walked together into the hall, where Frithjof was to see many things new to him. The walls, instead of bare, rough-hewn planks, were covered with hangings of gilt leather stamped with many cunning designs, of grapes and vines. Instead of a deep hearth in the middle of the floor, the huge logs blazed in fireplaces at both ends of the hall, with marble mantels. No smoke remained inside; no soot blackened the walls. The window had panes of glass; the door a· lock. And silver sconces stretched out their arms, laden with wax lights, instead of the smoky but fragrant pine chips, stuck in chinks of the planking. On a round table to itself there stood a deer roasted whole, with gilt hoofs and green boughs twined in his antlers. By each reveller's chair stood a handmaid, lily-cheeked and rosy-lipped, of golden locks or brown, of dark or azure eye, prompt in willing service.

High on a dais, in a chair of massive silver, the Earl sat in state; his golden helmet flashing light, his corslet too of gold; star-broidered his purple mantle's ample folds, bordered with a broad band of ermine.

He rose, and took three steps to meet his guest, with cordial hand outstretched.

"Take time to rest, I pray," he said after the first greeting, with kindly care. "Many a beaker have I drained with Thorsten, here in this very hall. His son, whose name, though young, is honoured far and wide, shall not sit far from me."

With his own hand the Earl filled a goblet with wine of Sicily, hot as flame and foaming as the sea-wave.

"Welcome in my own hall, son of my friend! This cup to hero Thorsten's memory!"

A Skald of high renown now tuned his harp. In low and solemn strains he pitched his song at first, then rose to loud and martial notes in praise of Thorsten's deeds.

And now the Earl plied his guest with many questions; Frithjof gave answer in words well chosen and discreet. He told of his perilous voyage, and how he had defeated the royal wizard's craft. Loud laughed the warriors; Angantyr smiled, well pleased; Frithjof had found favour with them all. But when he told of Ingeborg, so fair in her sorrow, so sweet in her thoughtfulness, eyes softened and lips ceased to smile; sighs came from many a gentle bosom, and of the maidens many would have liked to press so true a lover's hand.

At last he boldly told his mission. The Earl heard him patiently to the end, unmoved—or so it seemed. A silence fell on all.

"Tribute I never paid," he answered quietly. "I held Bele in honour, but never was vassal of his. As to his heirs, I know nothing of them. If they have a claim, let them be men and enforce it with the sword. We shall know how to meet them. But Thorsten was my friend."

He signed to his daughter who sat by his side. She understood the unspoken command and ran to her own chamber, whence she quickly returned and handed her father a belt-pouch. It was beautifully worked in green silk, the clasp set with rubies, the tassel of spun gold. The Earl filled it as full as it could hold with gold coined in many lands.

"This is for welcome,—my gift to my old friend's son," he said as he placed it in Frithjof's hand. "Do with it as thou pleasest. But stay with us the winter, I pray, and rest thee with thy men. The time for storms will soon be coming, and I would wager Ham and Heid will come to life again. Ellide may not always leap with such true aim, nor is there lack of whales for one that sank."

With talk and jest thus passed the night away. Cheerily the horn travelled round the board, yet the men kept well within bounds, and it was with clear heads and ringing voices that, just as day was breaking, the parting toast, " Earl Angantyr ! " was given out and drunk.

Frithjof stayed and had a pleasant winter.

XI

FRITHJOF'S RETURN

AT the first breath of spring in the blue air, at the first touch of green in the thawing fields, Frithjof thanked his host and once again trusted himself to the treacherous sea, now smooth and mild enough, and merrily Ellide drew the silver furrow across the dark blue plain. Light west winds sung in the sails like nightingales and Ægir's daughters, disporting themselves in their native waves, seemed playfully to help the ship along. 'T is joy to the mariner to set the sails for home, to watch for the smoke which rises from his own hearth, for the green mounds in which his fathers rest, for the rock from which a faithful maid has daily looked out on the sea.

Six days the voyage lasted, unhindered and unclouded. On the seventh a faint bluish streak is espied; it grows and expands into the jagged lines of rocky islets, and, at last, of solid land. Frithjof looks with beating heart, with dimming eye: 't is his own land, and those are his own woods; and now he can hear the waterfall which rushes headlong down the rock's naked breast. He greets the fjord, the headland; he sails hard by the temple and the grove where, last summer, he and Ingeborg talked and dreamed so many a night away.

"Why does she not come forth?" he thinks, impatiently. "Can she not feel how near I am to her? or has she gone from Balder's keeping, and does she sorrowfully spend her days in Helge's home, between the harp, the distaff, and the loom?"

And lo! from the temple's roof his favourite falcon comes flying with joyful shriek and lights upon his shoulder, as was his wont. He flaps and flaps his snowy wings, holds fast the shoulder, scratches with his claw in wild excitement, and pecks with his bill in Frithjof's ear with little moaning cries, as though he would quickly tell him something of import.

Ellide now lightly turns the point; 't is as though her keel felt the touch of native waters. Frithjof stands at the prow and looks eagerly towards the shore. He rubs his eyes and holds his hand over them—in vain! there is no sign of his own Framnäs. Yet stay! a tall chimney-stack, bare and black, rises in the middle of a heap of rubbish—cinders, ashes, stones. He looks, and looks again—his heart stands still—he leaps ashore, strides to where the gate once stood—the house, the barns: a waste! no sign of life! Only his hound, his faithful Bran, who has worried many a bear for him, runs out and springs at him in wild glee, baying and whining; and his favourite courser, milk-white, with golden mane, swan-necked and deer-footed, comes bounding from the wood, neighing and whinnying, and nibbles at his hand for bread. Alas! Frithjof now is poorer than these friends; he has nothing more to share with them, not even the shelter of a roof!

He does not know how long he stands upon his wasted homestead's land, when, turning round, he finds Hilding, his aged foster-father, by his side. He has no greeting for the old man in the great bitterness of his soul, but gives vent to his anger at once:

"What I now behold I might have foreseen. The eagle flown, they robbed the nest. A truly royal feat! However, it angers me more than it grieves. Now tell me, where is Ingeborg?"

"I will tell thee," replied Hilding, "for thou must know sometime. But I fear me the tidings will not please thee. No sooner hadst thou gone, than Ring came on in force. There was a battle—only one. King Halfdan, boyish in manner as ever, laughed and jested, yet when it came to fighting, showed himself a man. But there was not much fighting, for Helge lost heart and fled—and that was the end. As he passed thy homestead in his flight, he set fire to it. Now the brothers had no choice: Ring would accept of no peace-offering but their sister. If not—he would take their land and crown. There was much parleying; many messages went back and forward: but——well, King Ring has his bride."

"Oh women, women!" cried Frithjof, passionately. "Out on their rosy cheeks, whose blush is a lie! their laughing eyes, whose loving glance is deceit! their dainty lips, whose smile is perjury! They do say of Balder's Nanna, she was true. But then she was a goddess. There is no truth in human souls, if Ingeborg could be false. False—yet how dear! As far back as memory takes me, she was my one thought, my one desire, my mate in earnest and in play; of all the deeds I dreamed of doing, she was to have been the prize. I cannot, cannot think of myself apart from her. Yet here I stand—alone! Away! away! I will not think of her again, the fair witch, the bride that played me false! Away with dalliance and with dreams! I will out into the world, wherever there is food for my sword, on mountain height, in peopled valley, or on ocean wave. Let me but meet a king —see if I spare him! And if, between scenes of tempest and of slaughter, I should haply chance upon some love-sick boy, from very pity, by my troth, I will slay him straight, and save him from standing some day, betrayed, bereft, befooled—as I stand here!"

"How rash and reckless courses youthful blood!" sighed Hilding. "It takes the snows of age to cool it. Thou dost wrong the noble maid most grievously. Sorrowful she dwelt in Helge's house. To me alone she opened all her heart; I alone knew how bravely that gentle spirit battled with its grief. 'I am the victim of expiation,' she often said to me, 'that is to ransom my country and my people. I might die, 't is true; but a harder lot was set aside for me. What I am going to is a lingering death in life. But, father, tell no one of my agony. Suffering I can accept, but not compassion;—the King's daughter recoils from that. . . . But to Frithjof take the greet- of poor Ingeborg!' On the wedding-day —oh that it had never dawned!—the men-at-arms, the maiden's own body-guard, walked to the temple two by two. Sadly stepped the Skald with his harp before the sable steed, on which the bride sat pale as a spirit on a dark thundercloud. In these my arms I lifted her from the saddle, slender and swaying as a lily-stalk, and led her in. Yet she took the vow with voice both firm and clear. All were in tears, except herself. Only one ugly incident marred the dignity of the sad and solemn rite: King Helge caught sight of thy ring upon her arm, and tore it off roughly, with a curse. Now, by her wish, it is on Balder's arm, and in his sacred keeping. My patience at this gave way; I snatched my sword from my side—the King's life was not worth much to me just then. But Ingeborg whispered: 'Let go the sword! True, a brother might have spared me this; but the heart will bear much before it breaks. All-Father shall requite. I murmur not.'"

"All-Father shall requite!" Frithjof broke in. "Methinks it would please me to do a little of the requiting myself. Is not this Balder's Midsummer day? Yonder in the temple the priestly king will be holding high revelry—the murderer, the incendiary, who trades away his sister-ward. The very thing! I feel inspired to play the judge!"

XII

BALDER'S FUNERAL PYRE

THE Midnight Sun stands over the hills, blood-red and beamless. It is not day, it is not night—a something grey and weird. Balder's funeral pyre, emblem of the Sun, is burning on the hearth. When it is all burned down, winter's reign begins on earth.

The priests were busy with the fire—pale old men with flowing silver locks, holding knives of flint in horny hands. Not far from them stood Helge, the crown on his head, ministering at the altar-stone. When, hark! the clang of arms was heard from the sacred grove, and a voice in stern command:

"Björn, keep watch here at the gate. They are in the trap—let not one escape; kill them first, every one."

Helge stood pale, as turned to stone:
too well he knew that voice. Frithjof
entered, like an angry god, and his voice
was like the storm's:

"Here the tribute! I fetched it for
thee from beyond the seas. Take it!
Then, here by Balder's pyre, we fight for
life or death. Shield on back, and open
breast! That is the way to fight. Thine,
as King, be the first stroke; the second
shall be mine. Look not so anxiously
at the door! Rather think of Framnäs!
Think too of Ingeborg, the golden-
locked!"

He spoke, and taking from his belt the
heavy purse, hurled it with aim deliberate
straight at Helge's head. Blood spurted
from the royal nose and mouth, the knees
gave way, and, senseless, pale, by the altar-stone lay the grandson of the gods.

"What!" mocked Frithjof; "not stand
the touch of thine own gold? Thou most
dastardly of Norseland's sons! Angurwadel would scorn to draw blood from
such as thou. Quiet, priests! Down with
the sacred knives, ye phantom shapes of

night! Else are ye ripe for death—our blades are all athirst. And thou, pale Balder, check thy anger, for, by thy leave, I must have that ring upon thine arm—'t was never meant for thee. Not for thee, I dare maintain, did Waulund shape the gold. Stolen goods, taken from weeping maid, are no fitting gift for gods!"

As he spoke, he reached for the ring and would have stripped it off the statue's arm; but pull and tug as he would, ring and arm seemed grown together; and when at last the ring came off, the statue swayed with the wrench and fell headlong into the fire. In a twinkling the flame caught at the beams of the roof—Björn at the door grew deadly pale, and Frithjof stood transfixed. But not for long. Seized with horror at the sacrilege, at his own unwilling deed, his one thought was now to save.

"Wide the doors!" he cries. "Get out the people! Take off the watch! The temple burns! Water!—pour water! pour the sea!"

A chain is quickly formed from the temple to the beach; buckets run from hand to hand; the water hisses and sputters on the heated wood. Frithjof sits astride of the roof and floods it as the buckets reach him; his voice never ceases ringing out commands; he alone directs the work, and holds his dangerous post, heedless of the encompassing flames and smoke. But nothing helps—not his almost insane bravery, nor his men's untiring efforts. The gold and silver plating melt as in a smelting furnace, and the liquid metal falls in heavy drops upon the sand.

All is lost! Many did say afterwards that they saw a fire-red cock fly out of the flames, and stand on the top of the roof, crowing and flapping his wings. A brisk northerly wind quickened still more the work of destruction; from the temple the flames leaped over to the grove, hungrier for the lavish food. How they raged among the boughs! how they licked the curling, shrivelling foliage up! With a roar as of the tempest they swept through the summits; they bored their way into the earth, and the roots cracked and smouldered. The grove, but now a standing sea of fire, suddenly collapsed into a wilderness of glowing stumps, and a vast heap of red cinders and ashes.

The battle has long been given up. And when the early summer morning ruthlessly shows the night's awful work, the people silently disperse. But Frithjof goes his way alone, weeping the scalding tears of a strong man's despair.

XIII

FRITHJOF THE VIKING

IT was another summer night, soon after the temple fire, and Frithjof, restless, sleepless, was pacing the deck of his ship; and as he paced it, his eye clung to the shore; he sought out each dear, familiar spot, from his father's mound to the rock streaked with the waterfall's silver, and took silent leave from them—forever. For this was his last night in his native land, his native waters. His sentence had been spoken by the King and approved by the people: banishment for life, and death at any hand, if found within the boundaries of the country, or a certain distance from shore. One course only was now open to him: to take Björn and a few trusty comrades, and let Ellide bear them out into the wide world,—to roam the seas at random, taking what came his way, bound by no tie of country, kin or friendship—outside his ship—the true sea-king's pirate life.

But he was not to depart unmolested. Helge's hatred was not so easily satisfied, and he set a trap for the man he had driven into crime. As Ellide warily and daintily threaded her way between cliffs and banks and was just coming out of the fjord into the open sea, she found herself confronted with ten of the King's finest dragon-ships, which had been placed so as to cut off her course and capture Frithjof within the prescribed distance. Helge himself was on one of them. His crews set up a derisive shout as they started to attack.

Then a thing happened, wonderful and awful to behold. Invisible forces fought Helge's dragons, invisible hands drew them down one by one into the deep with their crews, and the King alone succeeded in swimming ashore from one of the wrecks. A peal of laughter rang after him from Ellide's deck. It was Björn, rejoicing in his foresight and the clever trick he had played upon the foe. Ever alert, he had got wind of Helge's wicked scheme, and swimming up to each ship under water, under cover of the night, had quietly bored a hole in each hold, near the keel. His one regret now was that Helge should have escaped.

And now Ellide bore her small troop of desperate spirits, gallantly as the free-born falcon, across the unfrequented seas of the high North. Frithjof knew that he could not too soon establish some kind of orderly rule on board if he was to keep his men under control; so he set about composing a code of laws, by which he should be bound as well as they and which should be fair to all. That they should bind themselves of their own free will to certain laws of their own was absolutely necessary, since, being cast out of the protection which common law awards to other men, they could not be expected to respect it. The following are some of the points in this code:

"Sleep not in a tent on board or in a

house on land. Foes might lurk within. Sleep sword in hand, Viking, and be the blue sky thy tent.

"When it storms, set all sails. It is cowardly to take in the sails; perish first!

"When on land, protect women and maidens. But let them keep away from the ship. For Freya herself would deceive thee. The dimple in a fair cheek is the deadliest of traps, and a woman's flying locks are the strongest of nets.

"If thou dost meet a merchant man, protect his ship; but let him, who is weak, pay a toll to the strong. For thou art king of the sea, and he is the slave of profit. His gold is not worth more than thy steel.

"Profit and booty shall be divided on open deck by the fortune of dice, and whatever thy lot, do not thou complain. The Sea-King himself throws no dice—honour is his share.

"If another Viking's ship comes along, then grapple and fight. If thou yield but a hair's-breadth, thou art our comrade no more.

"But let victory content thee. He who sues for peace is like an unarmed man,—no longer a foe. A villain he who gives no heed to prayer.

"A wound is the Viking's pride and best ornament, if sported on the breast or brow. Though bleeding, bind it not 'fore night, or thy welcome is less at the feast."

These laws of Frithjof's making quickly became known far and wide. His deeds, his name, were on all men's lips. Some blessed, and some cursed it; among all the sea-kings of new or olden times, the like of him, people said, had not been seen.

But he himself sat ever by the rudder alone, looking gloomily down into the ever-shifting waves.

"Thou art deep," he thought, "and in thy depths there may be peace; but up here there surely is none. O Balder, thou bright one! if thou be wroth with me, then draw thy sword, and I will gladly fall on it. But no! he sits above the clouds, and sends me thoughts which darken my mind."

Only in the hour of battle his spirit rises, as soars the eagle after a span of rest. Then his brow clears, and his voice rings high, and he stands as Thor before his crew. And so he sailed from victory to victory over the waters' ever open grave.

One day he found himself in those very seas of Greece to which he once would have lured Ingeborg from their Northern home. And those seas, those isles, with their groves and ruins, just as his father described them, cast their spell on him for a while, and drew him strongly to remain. It was but a fleeting impulse; and, by a strange reaction, home-sickness for his rugged North overcame him among the allurements of the South as never before. Then he remembered that this was just what Ingeborg predicted. And his thoughts went back to her with a rush:

"Where is she now? Does she ever think of me by the side of her elderly lord? Ah! I can never forget. I would die—how willingly! to see her again, to see her just once! It is three years since

I last saw my own land: is it still as green and fair? Do the mountains still tower as lofty into the pale blue sky? On my father's grave I planted a young linden tree—has it prospered, I wonder? 't was but a tender thing. And who cares for it now? O earth, feed its roots, and, heaven, give it thy dew to drink!—— But why should I longer roam these foreign seas, and rob and kill for a pastime? Fame I have won enough, and as for gold—I despise the wretched trash. The flag at the mast points northward, and there lies the land I love. Yes! I will follow the wind, the herald of heaven! I will steer to my own, my native North!"

Having arrived at this decision, Frithjof opened his heart to his friend with his usual directness:

"Björn, I am sick of the sea. These everlasting moving waves are but wild company. My beloved North with its strong, firm rocks, draws me back. Ah, happy he who may dwell where his fathers rest! Too long have I wandered aimlessly, a miserable outlaw."

But Björn replied in his quiet, somewhat stolid way:

"The sea is good. There alone we find a merry life and free. When age comes, it will be time enough to take root in the earth, like the grass. Now I would rather fight and feast on board a good ship, and get all the pleasure I can out of my life."

Then Frithjof came out with what really was in his mind all the time:

"Dost remember how once the ice drove us to the land? How the waves froze about the keel? I will not miss another of our brave long winters, tarrying here among the cliffs of this lonely strand. Once more I want to feast in the North at the merry Yule-tide—and I will! as a guest of Ring, of my bride that was. I must look once more on the silken gold of her hair, listen once again to the witching music of her voice."

"I see," said practical Björn. "Ring is to be taught how swifter than lightning is a Viking's vengeance, as we set fire to his palace and carry the fair one away.

Or wouldst thou challenge him to single combat, with a fair field and no favour, on land or on the ice? That too were Viking's fashion. Speak! I am ready for either or any venture."

But Frithjof stopped him indignantly:

"Speak not to me of war, of killing and burning. I will visit the King in peaceful guise. I blame him not, nor his unwilling bride: 't was all the work of a god's avenging hand. There is nothing left for me on earth to hope for; I will take my leave of her who must ever be dear to me—a leave eternal. When the cattle are brought out to pasture—sooner perhaps—I shall be there."

Sentiment was the only thing Björn never could understand.

"Frithjof, I have no patience with such foolishness," he said roughly. "Where is the sense of sighing and whining about a woman? The world is full of them—more's the pity. For one whom you miss, you can catch a thousand. Why, only say the word, and I will fetch you a shipload of the cattle, straight from the South, red as roses, tame as lambs; we can share the cargo or take our chance by lots."

Despite his melancholy, Frithjof could not but laugh at his friend's quaint outburst.

"Björn," he said, "thou art open and honest as the day, wise in the council, brave in battle; Odin and Thor stand ever by thee; but Freya, the heaven-born, is a stranger to thee. Beware thou anger her not! There is a spark in each human breast—aye, and in gods—which must at some time wake into flame at her touch.

Arguing was not Björn's strong point. Besides, he saw that Frithjof's mind was made up and concern for his friend's safety drove other thoughts away. So he only said:

"Go not alone, at least. I should know no peace."

"I am not alone when my good sword is with me."

"Shouldst thou fall, brother, thou shalt be avenged; I can promise thee that."

"There will be no occasion," said Frithjof calmly. And so it was settled.

XIV

AN UNBIDDEN GUEST

'TWAS Yule-tide. King Ring, serene and gracious, sat at the head of his own festive board — never was kindlier host. And by him, fair and gentle, sat his queen: spring and autumn strangely mated.

When lo! a stranger stood in the door: an old man, wrapped in a bear's pelt to his feet, weak and bent, leaning on a knotty staff. Yet was he great of stature beyond all the assembled guests. He sat him down close by the door, the place for poor guests in all times. The company laughed and exchanged glances, and some pointed at him with their fingers.

The stranger's eyes shot forth blue lightning. With one hand he seized the nearest of the scoffers, a flippant, beardless youth,—and, seemingly without effort, stood him on his head. The others looked on in silence and gave no sign of anger, for each man thought to himself, " I should have done the same."

"What is the noise down there?" the King asked angrily. "Who is it breaks the peace? Come here, old man, speak up: what is thy name? thy country? what seek'st thou here?"

"Many questions in one breath, O King," said the stranger; "my answer shall be brief. My name is nothing to thee—'t will take care of itself. Misery is my country, want my patrimony. Yesternight I slept with the wolf; to-night I come to thee. There was a time, I rode merrily my good dragon-ship; it had strong wings and flew with tempest speed. Now 't is frozen fast and lies, a captive, by the strand. I wished to see the King whose wisdom is famed in many lands; but thy men jeered at me, and I am too old to put up with insults. So I took up one of the fools and turned him upside down. He took no harm and picked himself up straightway. No offence, O King!"

The King laughed.

"Not bad in sooth! I rather like thy coolness. And age has its privileges. Now come, sit thee down by me. And drop that clumsy disguise. Deceit of any sort ill suits with pleasure, and it is my will that pleasure reign at this festive time."

Then from the guest's head fell the shaggy pelt, and in the old man's place there stood a youth in all the splendour of manhood. From the high brow down to the broad shoulders flowed the wealth of golden locks. A blue velvet mantle thrown back from the breast set off the silver belt, broad as a man's hand, on which, in high chased work, was seen a hunt, with flying hart and pursuing hounds. Broad bands of gold glistened on the arms, and the sword—sheathed lightning!—fell idly on one side. Thus the hero stood revealed. His eye, now mild and thoughtful, took in the hall, the hosts, and the guests. Tall as Thor, fair as Balder, he stood before the King.

Into the Queen's pale cheeks the blood shot quickly at the sight; a snowfield thus is flushed with a reflection of the Northern Light; and her breast could be seen heaving through the clinging robe.

But hark! a horn's blast loud and long sounded through the hall. All talk ceased at the signal, for it ushered in the most solemn ceremony of Yule-night,—the taking of vows for the coming year.

Amid a profound, reverent silence, the boar was brought in, the emblem of Frey, the Sun-god, who from this, the longest night of the year, begins to gather strength to overcome the evil brood of winter giants. The boar was a mighty forest beast, skilfully roasted whole, with wreaths of evergreens around his neck and shoulders, and an apple in his mouth. As the bearers set the heavy burden down, the King and all his guests bent the knee.

King Ring was the first to rise and touch the boar's brow. This was the vow he took;

"I will find and capture Frithjof, even though there be no champion to compare with him. So help me Frey, and Odin, and mighty Thor!"

With scornful laugh the unknown sprang from his knees to his full height, his eyes flashed wrathfully, and his features worked angrily. He struck his sword against the table with such violence as made the walls resound and every guest start to his feet.

"Hear now *my* vow, my lord King," he cried. "I know Frithjof well; he and I are blood-kin. I will defend him, though a world rise up in arms against him. So help me Fate and my good sword!"

The King laughed good-naturedly, and said:

"I call that a challenge if ever there was one. But speech is free where King Ring rules. Come, my Queen, pour out a horn of wine for our touchy guest, of our best. He will, I trust, remain with us all winter."

The Queen took up the horn that stood upon the table before her, on bright silver feet, mounted with hoops of gold, filled it

QUEEN AND VIKING.

to the brim, and offered it to the guest, with downcast eye; but it trembled as she held it, and a few red drops were spilt upon her lily-white hand. He took it gently from her and raised it to his lips. As men are now, no two would have drained that horn; he smiled, and quaffed it at one draught.

Then the Skald took the harp which stood by the royal table, and sang of love and war, of ancient fathers' deeds on land and sea, and of Valhalla's joys, and all that men delight to hear at feasts, while still the mighty horn went on its frequent rounds. High ran the revel and harmless merriment, and when the guests dispersed, their sleep was deep and free from care.

XV

ON THE ICE

FRITHJOF made no formal promise in reply to the old King's cordial invitation, but he staid from day to day, most likely uncertain in his own mind as to his further actions. Had Ingeborg known him when he threw off his disguise and stood before her motionless for a long moment, almost challenging her with his fixed look? This was the only question which occupied him, and he could not decide it to his satisfaction. At all events, she had not betrayed herself; not a glance ever passed between them other than was natural between hostess and guest—not a word that might have been construed into double meaning. A stern feeling of honour kept him under close control, so that their intercourse almost might have been called unrestrained. Was it pleasure, was it pain such nearness gave him? He could hardly have told himself, the two feelings were so mixed. Anyhow, it would have been hard to tear himself away, and still he put off any positive decision.

Meanwhile, the old King appeared to take more and more delight in his guest's society. He would hear of no amusement, no excursion without him, and Frithjof could not possibly have kept aloof without ungraciousness, and indeed without exciting suspicion. On one occasion, it was well for the King and Queen that such was the former's fancy. A sleighing and skating expedition across the fjord was the order of the day. King Ring himself was driving his famous Swedish trotter, with Ingeborg in her nest of furs by his side, for she was fond of the exercise. Frithjof had strapped on his skates, and raced the trotter, to the court's amazement and delight. When suddenly there was a shriek of horror: sleigh and horse had broken through a thin spot on the ice and had almost disappeared. But before they could be sucked by the current under the ice, Frithjof, swift as lightning, was on the spot, just in time to grasp the horse's head at the bit, and with one pull, such as no other man could have given, had him out and on his feet, when he helped him drag the sleigh with its precious human load beyond the line of danger.

"That was a good pull, and strong!" the King cried admiringly. "Frithjof himself could not have done better."

All returned to the palace at once— there had been enough excitement for one day. And now the King pressed Frithjof so earnestly, that he at last pledged himself to remain at least until spring.

XVI

THE TEMPTATION

AND spring came in due time, and with it the chirping of birds, and the woodland foliage, and the long, long days. Once more the rivers ran, blithely singing, to the sea, glad of their liberty, and the human breast expanded with the renewed vigour of life and hope and joyousness.

A great hunt had long been planned to open the season. The Queen was to take part in it, and the whole court gathered in high spirits. Bows creak, arrows rattle in the quivers, the steeds paw the ground with impatient hoof, and the hooded falcons shriek with longing for a flight.

Now she appears, for whom all wait—the Lady of the Hunt. Alas, poor Frithjof, better look away! As the morning star rides a summer cloud, so light she sits her snowy palfrey. Canst thou bear to look upon those locks of gold thy hand so often stroked, those eyes whose azure was thy heaven, that graceful form which timidly clung to thee? Ah, no! look not that way, nor stay where thou canst hear that voice, sweet as the spring's own breath!

All is ready—they are off! Over mount and dale, heigho! The horns blow, the falcons soar straight up, as though they would storm Odin's own heaven; the woodland beasts fly terrified, and make for cave and den and burrow.

The aged King cannot follow at such speed. Frithjof alone rides by his side, silent and moody. His thoughts are far away.

"Why," he thinks, "why did I leave the sea, to my own harm and sorrow! Out there, where the waves play wild and free, there is no room for brooding, and if dark thoughts do come up, the winds of heaven blow them away, or else they yield to the cares of war. But here they flap their black pinions in my very face, and I go about as in a bad dream all day. Meseems I still walk in Balder's grove, still hear the words with which she swore me troth. She broke the oath——Ah, no! not she, not she! Angry gods—they broke it. They took my rosebud and laid it at Winter's breast. And is she any good to him? Winter knows not such a flower's worth, and his chilling breath clothes both bud and leaf, and stalk in ice."

Thus dreaming, Frithjof forgot himself, his host, the world. He rode on because his horse carried him, and noted not the quiet valley nestling among wooded slopes, shaded by ancient elms and birches, into which they had strayed, so that he started to hear the King's voice close to him:

"This is a lovely spot, and the grove is cool. Let us rest here, for I am tired. I fain would sleep awhile."

"Not here, O King! This is no spot for sleep. The ground is cold and damp; thou wouldst find unwholesome rest. Come, I will ride home with thee."

"Sleep, like other gods, sends his gifts unasked," said the King. "Wouldst grudge thy host a moment's rest?"

Frithjof then unfastened his mantle, and spread it on the ground; the old King laid his head upon his knees, and soon lay slumbering as sweetly as the warrior on his shield after a day of toil and battle, or as a child on its mother's arm.

And as he slumbers—hark! a black bird sings in the tree:

"Haste, Frithjof, strike! A single blow ends the strife. Then take the Queen—she is thine; for did she not give thee first a bride's kiss? No human eye sees thee, and dead men tell no tales."

Frithjof listens. Hark! a white bird sings in the tree:

"If no human eye can see thee, still Odin's eye is upon thee. Villain! wouldst thou murder sleep? The man is old, unarmed. Whatever thou mayest win, 't will not be glory surely."

Thus by turns the two birds sang, till Frithjof drew his sword, horrified, and flung it from him with such violence that it cut its way through the foliage and fell far into the wood. The black bird flew away to Nastrand, the black river of death. The white bird soared on light pinion high up into the sunlight, and its joyful carol was like the tone of a silver harp.

The old King woke up abruptly.

"This sleep is worth much to me," he said. "It is sweet to slumber in the shady grove, secure under the guard of a brave man's sword. . . . But, stranger, where *is* thy sword, own brother to the lightning? Speak! Who parted them that never should be parted?"

"I do not care," replied Frithjof. "There are swords enough in Norseland. A sword, O King, is sharp of tongue and seldom counsels well. Dark spirits lurk in steel—the whole black pack of hell. Sleep is not safe from them, and silver hair attracts them."

"Hear, then, O youth: I did not sleep. I but wished to test thee. A wise man never trusts to man or blade before he has made trial of both and found them true. Thou art Frithjof. I knew thee from the moment thou didst enter the hall. Old Ring has known all the time what thou didst so cleverly conceal, thou wary guest. Why didst thou steal into my home, disguised, nameless? Because thy intent was to rob the old man of his bride? Honour, Frithjof, never sits down at a man's board a nameless guest. I had heard much of one named Frithjof, a foe to the gods, a terror to men, a desperate man, burner of temples, a hero in war. Long I waited for him to come with an army and challenge me. Instead of which he comes in beggar's garb, with a beggar's staff. Nay, look not so shamed. I too have known the ardour of youth. I tried thee—and forgave. I pitied—and forgot. Look on me: I am old, ripe for the grave. When I am gone, take thou my realm, take my Queen—she is thine by right. Till then bide with me still, and be my son. The feud between us is no more."

If Frithjof was astonished at what the King told him, he did not show it, but replied gloomily:

"I did not come as a thief. Had I meant to take thy wife from thee, say—who could have hindered me? No! I only longed to see once more her who had been my promised wife; once, only once, and, alas! for the last time. Ah, woe is me! Flames half extinguished I fanned into a new blaze, and it consumes me. Too long, O King, have I tarried; I must go. The wrath of gods unreconciled lies too heavily on my outlawed head. Balder of the shining locks, who looks on all things with love, hates me alone, the banished outcast!—Yes, I did set fire to the temple. For that am I now called 'the Wolf.' Children shriek at my name, and revellers are dumb. There is no peace for me at home, none within my own breast. The green earth has no place for me. The ground burns under my feet, the tree gives me no grateful shade. Ingeborg is lost to me; my life's sun has set, darkness wraps me round. Then ho, to sea! Thy black breast, my dragon, bathe once more in the salt sea-waves! Spread thy wings to the gale, plough up the waters, fly to the uttermost end, so far as stars will guide and winds will carry thee! Let me hear once more the turmoil of the storm, once more feel the fury of battle—in the midst of chaos calm may descend into my breast."

XVII

KING RING'S DEATH

THE next morning, as Skinfax, the Sun-steed with the golden mane, emerged from the waves in the East, and the first rays of morn gilded the roof of the banquet-hall, there was a knock at the gate. With careworn brow, but firm tread, Frithjof entered and approached the place where sat the King, thoughtful and silent, and Ingeborg, pale and agitated. The guest began his farewell speech in a voice unlike his own, it was so low and broken:

"The time has come. Wind and tide serve. I must go from my friends and the land of my love. Ingeborg, take back my arm-ring, be it a sacred token to thee, never part with it. From my heart

I forgive, but never on earth shalt thou see me again. Never again will I look at smoke that rises in the North. Home and grave I will find in the sea. King Ring! never go with the women to walk on the beach! especially not on starlit nights. Thou mightst behold, driven to land, Frithjof, the outlawed Viking's, corpse."

But the King would hear no more:

"It ill beseems a man to whimper like a love-sick girl. The death-song is heard all over the world; I too have heard it; —what of that? must not all things that live go the way of death? What is decreed must be, and neither plaint avails, nor raving against fate. Frithjof, what I said to thee, I say again: I give thee wife and land; take care of them for my infant son. Nothing have I so loved, for nothing striven so, as peace—golden, happy peace; yet have I broken shields and lances with the best, on sea and land, and no one ever saw my cheek to blanch. But I would not willingly die the straw-death,[1]

---

[1] It was considered inglorious for Norse warriors to die from old age or disease. Such a death, derisively called the

the first of Norseland's rulers. It is not hard to part from life: far harder 't is to live than die." He said; and with his sword firmly cut the death-runes on his breast and arm; for a moment he watched the blood flowing warm and free, then called for a last horn of mead, Norseland's national drink.

"To thee I drink, to thy glory, O peerless North!" he spoke with voice still strong and firm. "In the midst of wild, bloodthirsty comrades I sought for peace—she never staid long with me! Now perchance I may find her in her heavenly home——Hail, ye gods, sons of Valhalla!——The earth goes from me——Welcome, ye Asas, the willing guest!"——

Once more he pressed Ingeborg's hands, his weeping friend's, and his little son's; then his eye broke, and in a sigh his spirit, freed, was wafted to All-Father's throne.

"straw-death," in scornful allusion to the couch or deathbed, deprived them of the right to enter Valhalla and share the joys of the warriors slain in battle and brought to Odin's hall by the Valkyries. Rather than forfeit this supreme privilege, aged warriors slew themselves with their own swords, when there was absolutely no prospect of their dying the honourable death of the battlefield,

XVIII

THE ELECTION

"TO the Ting! to the Ting!" With the call the herald goes from farm to farm, from home to home. King Ring is dead. Deep in the mound, in the spacious stone-lined chamber, he sits in state, the sword at his side, the shield on his arm, and his favourite charger faithfully waits to take him, fleet as ever, through spirit-land. And now a king must be chosen anew.

Each bonder takes his sword from the wall, carefully tries the edge and rubs the blade, while eager boys look on, then attempt to lift the weapon: two will do it; 't is too much for one. The daughter meanwhile cleans and polishes the helmet, and blushes as shs sees her own fair face reflected in the steel. Last comes the shield,—and ready stands, for deeds of peace or war, the true-hearted bonder, the free-born Norseman! 'T is in the breast of such as he that the nation's honour is safely housed. In peace he is his country's wise adviser, in war her stalwart champion ever.

In an open field, under the blue canopy, the men assemble with crash of shields and clash of arms. Frithjof stands straight and tall upon the judgment-stone, and close to him the little gold-haired lad, the old King's only son.

A murmur goes through the circle of men:

"Too young! No judge of men is he, nor fit to lead in war."

But Frithjof raises the child upon his shield:

"Behold your King! The country's blooming hope! Beauteous and noble of bearing as an infant Odin! See how light and well at ease he stands, poised on the unsteady shield! My sword shall guard his kingdom's honour and his own, and on his brow my hand shall place some day his father's crown. Forsete, Balder's son, keeper divine of justice and of men's faith—hear thou my oath, and if I break it, let my life pay the forfeit!"

Standing on the shield held high by the hero's outstretched arms, the child looks up with eye so bold as on the sun looks the young eagle. But soon he tires of the novel game and, with fearlessness right royal, leaps down upon the ground. With a roar of delight the Ting greets the daring feat, and the men cry out as one:

"We choose thee King! Be as thy father great and good! And let Frithjof in thy place rule until thou growest strong in mind and body! Earl Frithjof, hail! and take the mother for thy bride!"

But Frithjof spoke out loud and stern:

"This is election day, not wedding day that I know. Nor shall any man choose a bride for me. But I must now haste me to Balder's grove. My fate has waited there for me this many a day. Unreconciled as yet is the god of the golden locks.

He took my bride from me, and he alone can give her back."

He kisses the little King's brow in homage and greeting, and forthwith, alone and silent, they see him stride across the heath as one in haste.

XIX

THE VISION

IT was a glorious evening following on one of those perfect days in our early Northern spring, when nature seems to make the most of every hour to efface all signs of winter's long reign. Frithjof stood upon his father's mound and let his eyes wander leisurely from point to point of the beautiful landscape. The whole scene was so sweetly familiar in the golden light of the hour just before sunset, each well-loved landmark—of tree, and stream, and rock—stood out so clear and peaceful, that he found himself living again those days which he had for years, in his fierce and bitter grief, striven—how vainly!—to forget. "Unchanged are all things, save I alone!" That was the burden of his thoughts, the cry of his heart—and how passionately he wished the last few years away!

One feature of the scene, indeed, was new—and from that he had shudderingly turned away: the blackened, desolate spot where Balder's temple had stood, with the stately surrounding grove. But now he turned resolutely towards it, and looked full at the mutely accusing ruins.

"Oh!" he cried in despairing longing, "is there no such thing as forgiveness in Odin's heaven? A man whose friend was slain takes blood-money and forgives. The gods accept men's sacrifices. And thou, great Balder, can nothing pacify thy wrath? Yet men do say thou art the mildest of them all. And, knowing all things, thou must know that I never meant to burn thy house. Have mercy, then, and take the stain from my dishonoured shield! Lift from me the burden which is more than I can bear, and disperse the spirits of darkness which beset me! Cannot repentance and a blameless life atone for one moment's madness?"

He threw himself upon the mound as he would have thrown himself upon his father's breast.

"Dost sleep, my father?" he whispered. "But no! thou sittest, guest of the gods, at Odin's board, where voices from the earth may never reach thee. Yet, father, this once look down from those blessed abodes above the stars: thy son it is that calls thee—thee, Thorsten Vikingson. Give me but a sign! a word! How can I win great Balder's pardon?"

He sank, exhausted, on the grass. The sun was just setting in a golden sea; the evening breeze, softly rustling through the trees, sang its gentle lullaby to the weary man; sleep touched his brow with pitying hand, and the peace he sought so passionately came to him at last.

And in his sleep he saw a vision. A strange splendour seemed to descend from the darkening heavens, a mist of gold and purple, irradiated with a light not of this world. And slowly the glory took shape, and a wondrous aërial structure stood before the sleeper's spirit-sight, upon the rock where Balder's temple had been: high walls of silver, pillars of brass, an altar of a single precious stone. The dome, high and rounded, hung free above, as held by unseen hands, a half sphere of crystal, pure and blue as virgin ice or as the winter sky; and through the crystal were seen Valhalla's gods, seated on thrones in azure mantles and golden crowns. In the temple's wide-open portal stood the three Norns, the sister-Fates,— with the shield on which, in heavenly runes, are writ all things that have been, are, and are to be,—of countenance grave, yet mild withal and wondrous fair; Urda, the sister of the Past, pointing to the ruins of the old temple, and Skulda, the sister of the Future, to the vision of the new temple. Frithjof gazed in awe, admiring, and ere he could gather his sleep-bound wits the marvel had vanished. But as he woke he knew his prayer had been answered.

"The sign!" he cried. "Father, the sign from thee! I am to rebuild Balder's temple, fairer than it was, on the same spot. Oh joy, that 't is given me to atone!

The outcast may hope once more; the divine arms will open for him at last. Hail, ye stars! once more, with peace at my heart, I may watch your course. And hail, my native Northern Light! once more I may look on thy fiery beauty, nor think of burning temples. Now, father, I will lay me down, and while away this blessed night with dreams of human love and mercy all divine."

XX

RECONCILIATION

THE new temple was completed. The enclosure was not, as formerly, a mere wooden paling, but a railing of iron, with a gilt brass knob on each spike. The temple itself was built of huge quarry stones, a work for all eternity, yielding in nothing to that mighty temple at Upsala, in which Norseland sees the earthly counterpart of its own Valhalla. It towered on a beetling rock, mirrored in the still waters of the bay. And back of it, like a well tended garden, stretched the valley, and farther still the grove, alive with the song of birds. The portals were of brass, and, within, two mighty pillars upbore the dome's majestic sphere, which on the outside seemed a suspended giant shield of gold. The altar was hewn out of one solid block of Norseland's granite. And in the wall above was left an open space, deep blue with golden stars—there sat the silver statue of the god.

Such the temple. And this the morning of the consecration.

Two by two, twelve maidens entered, richly robed in cloth of silver, the bloom of roses on their cheeks and in their innocent hearts. In graceful, stately dance they moved around the altar, as woodland fairies dance on the grassy rounds, while morning dew yet sparkles on each blade and stalk; and, as they danced, they sang the sacred lay of Balder: how he was loved of gods and men, and all things breathing or inanimate in all the world, save only Loki, the malignant half-breed offspring of a Troll father and an obscure mother; how he fell, pierced by a toy arrow sent in sport by his blind brother Höder, but directed by Loki's evil hand; and how earth and sea and heavens wept for him.

Frithjof stood by, leaning on his sword,

spell-bound. It was as though his days of Viking life, with all their lawlessness and strife, were passing from him, and sinking, a bloody spectre, into the night of things forgotten, while the joys and dreams of his harmless boyhood came trooping round him, blue-eyed, flower-crowned, and smiled and beckoned to him with sweet familiar gesture. Higher and higher his soul felt lifted above these lowly haunts of human hatred, human vengeance; one by one the iron bands fell off that held his breast oppressed, as winter's ice melts from the frowning rock. The sunshine of peace and love flooded the hero's heart, which seemed to throb with the universal pulse—he could have held the world in fond encircling arms.

Now entered Balder's high-priest. Not fair and youthful as the god, yet tall and of commanding presence, with silver beard flowing down to his girdle, and heaven's own graciousness in his mild and noble countenance. A hitherto unknown feeling of pious awe thrilled Frithjof's being; the eagle pinions on his helmet bent low before the aged priest, as the venerable lips uttered the words of greeting:

"Welcome, son Frithjof! I have looked for thee. For power misled into violence and misused, if so the man's nature be but noble, is sure to return to its senses some day, and unite with gentleness. Then harmony will reign, and the man's breast, in its own little circle, will be the reflection of the life divine. For power there must be to lend piety and goodness efficiency, since these without power were but a structure upon sand. Thou wouldst atone and be reconciled? Knowest thou the meaning of the words? To atone and be reconciled is to rise after a fall purer, better, than before. We offer sacrifices to the gods and call them 'atonement.' But they are only signs, symbols, not the thing itself. No external act, no man, can take the burden of guilt from thee. A man's atonement is within his own breast. I know of one sacrifice, dearer to the gods than rarest incense-perfume: it is thine own heart's hatred, thy thirst for vengeance. If thou canst not tame these

—if thou canst not forgive,—then hadst thou better stay away from Balder's fane. Then is this temple thou hast built of no good to thee. Balder's forgiveness cannot be bought with a few blocks of stone. There can be no reconciliation where peace is not. Be reconciled with thy foe and with thyself, and the Golden-locked One is, as of yore, thy friend.

"There was once, some say, another Balder, far away in the South, a virgin's son. All-Father sent him to make dark riddles clear, and rugged paths smooth. 'Peace' was his battle-cry, Love was his sword, the dove of Innocence sat on his silver helmet. Gentle was his life, gentle his teaching, gently he died, forgiving; and down there, among palms, his grave is shown. His word, they say, survives him, wanders still from vale to vale, softens hard hearts, joins hard hands, and founds upon a gentler earth a reign of peace. I do not know the doctrine well myself, but in my better hours I seem to feel it vaguely in my heart. And so does every man. Some day, I know, 't will come our way, with white dove-wings lightly hovering over all Norseland. O hail, thou happy race of men that then shalt drink at the new fount of light, which no dense cloud will obscure as now! Yet scorn not us who with unblinking eyes have sought the splendour of the Sun we knew. All-Father is One, but he has many heralds.

"Thou, Frithjof, hatest Bele's sons. For what? For that they would not give to the bonder's son their sister, the daughter of a race which traces its descent back to Valhalla's thrones. 'The accident of birth,' sayest thou, 'is not merit to be proud of.' But know, O youth, no man is proud of his merits; men take pride only in their luck, the gods' free gifts. Art thou not proud of thy heroic deeds, of thy superior might and sinews of steel? Yet are all these merits of thine? Not more than the King's birth is his own merit. Respect the pride of others, if thou wouldst claim respect for thy own pride. And now that King Helge is no more——"

"What!" Frithjof broke in, amazed: "Dead? King Helge? where, and how?"

"He was, as thou well knowest," replied the priest, "at war with the Finns, while thou wert building here. There in Finnland, upon a solitary rock, stood an ancient temple, dedicated to their god Jumala, but closed and forsaken this many a long year. Above the entrance there still remained a quaint old image of the god, tottering and threatening hourly to fall. Yet no one dared approach, either to steady or take it down, because of an old prophecy, dark of sense, but dreaded all the more, that 'he who first came near the temple, *would behold Jumala.*' Helge, hearing of the prophecy, went into one of his fits of rage and swore to pull the temple down. He himself dared the steep ascent, but found the door locked, and the huge rusty key stuck fast in the lock. Furiously then he seized and shook the half-rotten pillars; they gave way with a terrible crash, the image fell on the King's head, and killed him on the spot: *he had beheld Jumala!* The tidings were brought us last night by a swift messenger. Now Halfdan sits alone on Bele's throne. Offer him thy hand, sacrifice to the gods thy wrath: this sacrifice Balder and I, his priest, demand of thee, in token that thou dost seek reconciliation in all singleness of heart. If thou canst not do this, then is all thy penitence a mockery, then had the temple better been left unbuilt, and all my words are wasted breath."

Here Halfdan stepped across the brass threshold and, with a timid look which well became his boyish beauty, stood on one side, apart from the dread Sea-King, silent and expectant. Slowly Frithjof loosed from his belt the sword, the dagger too, and laid them on the altar; his gold-rimmed shield he leaned against it, then, unarmed, approached his boyhood's friend, so untowardly turned into a foe.

"In this our feud," he said in gentle accents, "he who first holds out his hand for peace is the winner."

King Halfdan, flushing with joy, ungloved his hand and laid it in that other hand, and the two, long-parted, joined in a new-made bond, as strong and firm as their native rocks. The aged priest now solemnly spoke the words which loosed the ban and took the curse from the head late doomed to lie with wolves. And even as he spoke, Ingeborg entered, in bridal robes and ermine mantle, many noble maidens following her as stars the moon. With happy tears she fell upon her brother's breast, and he gently placed her in Frithjof's arms. Then was performed the wedding rite, and, across Balder's altar, she gave her hand to the lover of her youth.

NOTE ON THE "FRITHJOF-SAGA"

PERHAPS one of the many charms of this beautiful story is that it is a story all by itself, unconnected with the mythical cycle of the Edda, with very little supernatural agency, and that only in externalities (the magic ship, the storm-giants); an entirely human, vivid picture of Norse life just before it was perturbed and changed by the advent of Christianity,—probably in the eighth century. Antiquarians are pretty well agreed that the Saga was written down, from old popular ballads, about 1300, and have little doubt that the groundwork is historical. Thorsten and Bele's mounds are still shown near the city of Bergen; so is the rocky headland on which the once famous temple of Balder stood; the country around Christiania is still called Hringa-rika, " the realm of Ring."

The Saga in its old-Norse version is so complete, even to the smallest incidents, that when Esaias Tegner, Sweden's national poet, took it in hand, he had nothing either to add or to omit, nothing to invent, but only to soften one or two crudenesses, and clothe the whole with the charm of his poetic conception, of his wonderful imagery and diction.

Folk-lore and popular epic poetry were not held in honour by the literary world of the beginning of this century: it was too much enthralled by the pseudo-classicism of the French culture of the last two centuries, and too much fascinated with the coldly rationalistic philosophy of which Voltaire and the Encyclopedists were the exponents. It is well known that their disciple, King Frederic the Great of Prussia, complained to one of his Paris correspondents that some fool of a bookworm had sent him some absurd old stories—trash which he would like to throw out of the window. The "trash" was the first modern-German version of the "Nibelungenlied." Patriotism had a good deal to do with the revival of folk-lore in the different Teutonic countries, and when men like the brothers Grimm and Karl Simrock in Germany collected nursery tales from the lips of peasant grandames or transcribed into modern-German prose and verse the old national songs, heroic legends, and epics, they avowedly followed up the national revolt against French political rule, by raising the country's intellectual self-consciousness and inciting it to revolt against the tyranny of French spiritual domination and literary fashion.

The same movement was taken up and fostered by Adam Œhlenschlæger and Esaias Tegner, the national poets of Denmark and Sweden, where both the partisanship and opposition were quite as vehement as in Germany, because if, in these remoter countries, the political yoke was not as directly oppressive, the spiritual thraldom was hardly less complete. At the present day it seems so natural that writers should take the subject-matter of their novels, dramas, poems, if not from contemporary life, then out of the national treasury of legend and history, that we can scarcely realize what a startling innovation were the first attempts in this direction. Fortunately, the innovators were the master minds of the time, which had the power to force a hearing and, once heard, to fascinate and to convince. This gift of fascination Tegner possessed in the highest degree, and, while he himself doubted his success, being naturally modest and diffident, and, in his letters to friends, expressed a fear lest he might have injured the cause of his beloved folk-legends by unskilful treatment of the particular Saga he had selected,—the poem took the country by storm and, in its further triumphant march, included not only the entire Northern world, but even the literary circles of remote nationalities. This is shown by the number of metrical translations of it in existence: twenty-one German and nearly as many English, several Danish, French, Dutch, Polish, Latin, and one Italian, one Russian, one Hungarian, one Greek, and one Icelandic.

As to the poet's own native Sweden, it is said that there is hardly a peasant's cabin where a copy of the *Frithjof-Saga* is not treasured by the side of the Bible and the Hymnal, the three mostly forming the entire family library. This is popularity indeed!

ROLAND

THE PALADIN OF FRANCE

"LA CHANSON DE ROLAND"
"THE LAY OF ROLAND"

Halt sunt li pui e mult halt les arbres.
   Quatre piruns i ad luisant de marbre.
Sur lerbe uerte li quens Roll se pasmet.
Vns sarrazins tute ueie lesguardet.
Si se feinst mort si gist entre les altres.
Del sanc luat sun cors e sun uisage.
Met sei en piez e de curre s'aistet.
Bels fut e forz e de grant uasselage.
Par sun orgoill cumencet mortel rage.
Roll saisit e sun cors e ses armes.
E dist un mot uencut est li nies carles.
Iceste espee porterai en arabe.
   En cel tireres li quens s'aperceut alques.
Ço sent Roll que s'espee li tolt.
Vurit les oilz si lad dit un mot.
M en escientre tu nies mie des noz.
Tient lolifan que unkes pdre ne uolt.
Sil fiert en lelme ki gemet fut a or.
Fruisset lacer e la teste e les os.
Amsdous les oilz del chef lei ad mis fors.
Jus a ses piez sil ad cresturnet mort.
Apres li dit culuert paien cu fus unkes si os.
Que me saisis ne a dreit ne a tort.
Ni ot raz hume ne te uenget por fol.
Fenduz en est mis olifans el gros.
Caiuz en est li cristals e li ors.
   Ço sent Roll la ueüe ad p̱due.
Met sei sur piez quanquil poet se suertuet.

FACSIMILE OF A PAGE OF THE "CHANSON DE ROLAND" (LAY OF ROLAND), FROM A MS. OF THE XIITH CENTURY NOW AT OXFORD, IN THE BODLEIAN LIBRARY.

PART FIRST

GANELON'S TREASON

I

KING MARSILIUS HOLDS A COUNCIL AT SARAGOSSA

CHARLES, the King and great Emperor, had been in Spain full seven years, and had conquered the highlands all the way to the sea. Not a castle could stand before him, not a city was left with walls unbroken, except Saragossa, which is on a mountain. King Marsilius held it himself,—the Paynim King who loved not God, but served Mahomet and Apollo.[1]

[1] Historical accuracy in details is not expected of these mediæval poets, the truth of whose work lies in the reproduction of character and the pictures of the life of given periods. This first paragraph is bristling with inaccuracies as

One morning he went into a shady orchard, where a couch of precious rugs and luxurious pillows had been spread for him on some marble steps. Over twenty thousand men stood round, waiting on his will. He called to him his dukes and counts and spoke to them as follows:

"Hear me, lords; hear what evil days have come upon us. Emperor Charles, the ruler of France, for our destruction has come into our land. I have no army left to do battle with him or to break up his own. Advise me then, ye my wise men and true: save me from death and shame."

The Paynim knights heard in blank distress; not one had a single word to say.

At last Blancandrin stepped forward, as one who would speak. He was, among

---

regards actual historical facts. Charlemagne had been in Spain only one year, not seven. He was not yet Emperor. He took that title in 800 A.D., while the disaster at Roncevaux happened in 778. The Moors or Saracens, the conquerors of Spain, were Mussulmans; and everybody knows that Mussulmans worship the one true God and follow the law of Mahomet, whom they hold in veneration as the Prophet of God. As for the Greek heathen god Apollo, they did not so much as know his name.

his peers, a man of great repute—a valiant knight and wise beyond the rest; always ready with good counsel, to help his liege lord in his needs.

"Be not dismayed even yet," he now said to the King. "Send to Charles, the proud, the haughty, with promises of faithful service and great friendship, and with gifts: bears, and lions, and hounds; seven hundred camels, falcons that have done moulting; of coined gold and silver four hundred mule-loads—enough to pay off his army. But tell him he has made war in this country long enough, and must return home, to his city of Aix; that you will follow him thither by St. Michael's feast, receive the Christian law, and be thenceforth his man, in all honour and truth. And if he asks for hostages, let him have them—ten, or even twenty, the better to assure him. Let us send our own sons; I will send mine, though it be to his death: better they should lose their heads, than that we here should lose our honour and our sovereignty, and be made beggars all together."

The Paynims listened and approved: "It were well done," they said.

Blancandrin went on:

"By this right hand, and by this beard which the breeze blows about my breast, you shall quickly see the French raise their camp and return to their own land. Charles, in his city of Aix, will celebrate St. Michael's Day with a great festival. The day will pass, the term set by you, with no sign of your coming; Charles is terrible in wrath, and unrelenting. He will cut off our hostages' heads. Still, it is better so than that we should lose fair Spain at last, and suffer endless woes and tribulations."

Again the Paynims approved: "Well may it be as he says."

King Marsilius now dismissed the council, and kept with him only Blancandrin and nine more of his most trusty knights, to impart to them his design.

"Lords," he began, "ye shall go to Charlemagne, where he now is encamped before Cordova, the great city, which he besieges. Ye will bear in your hands olive branches in token of peace and submission. If ye have craft enough to make my peace with him, ye shall have gold and silver, and land to your heart's content."

Quoth the Paynims: "Our liege speaks well."

"Say to Charles from me," Marsilius went on, "that for his God's sake he take pity on me; tell him that before a month has passed, I will join him with one thousand of my noblest knights, receive the Christian law, and be his man in all love and truth."

Said Blancandrin: "You will surely get a good treaty."

Marsilius then ordered ten white mules to be brought, which had been sent him some time before by the King of Sicily, with bits of gold and saddles of silver. These the ten messengers bestrode. With olive branches in their hands they appeared before Charles.

Let him look to himself! they will fool him yet.

II

CHARLEMAGNE HOLDS A COUNCIL AT CORDOVA

CHARLES was happy and in the best of humours. He had just taken Cordova, torn down the city walls, demolished the towers with his war engines. His knights had found much booty, in gold and silver, in precious garments and equipments. Not one man was left in the city but was either killed or baptised.

King Charles was taking his ease in a vast orchard. With him were his nephew Roland, and Oliver, the two inseparable friends, Duke Geoffrey of Anjou, and many more — fifteen thousand French knights in all. They were seated in groups on rugs and passed the time with games: some played at backgammon, the older and wiser ones played chess, the youngsters fenced. Under a pine, near a wild-rose bush, was a throne of solid gold: there the King sat, looking on, well pleased, of mighty stature and imperial bearing, with long white beard and snowy locks. If any asked for him, no need to point him out. The Paynim messengers, alighting from their mules, saluted him most humbly and presented the gifts sent by Marsilius. Their spokesman, Blancandrin, then repeated word for word the message with which he was entrusted.

The Emperor sat long in silence, with head bent low; for he was never hasty in his speech; it was his wont to take his time before he spoke. When at length he raised his brow, his countenance was hard and stern.

"Ye have spoken well," he said to the messengers. "But King Marsilius is my greatest foe: in how far, then, can I trust these words of yours?"

"You shall have noble hostages," replied the Saracen; "ten, fifteen, nay twenty. My own son shall be of the number, and there will be youths of birth still nobler. My master will follow you to Aix, where God has made the healing springs to spurt from the ground for you, and there, on the great feast of St. Michael, he will become a Christian and swear fealty to you."

"It is the only way in which he still can save himself," replied Charles.

It was a beautiful evening, with a cloudless sun. Charles ordered the ten mules taken to his own stables; then, in the great orchard, had a handsome pavilion set up for the messengers, who slept there under the guard of ten men-at-arms till it was bright daylight. Charles, who was an early riser, did not have them called, but was up himself at sunrise, heard matins and early mass, then sat down under the pine and summoned his barons to council; for he never took any important decision without consulting his French nobles. There were Ogier the Dane, and Richard of Normandy, Turpin the Archbishop of Rheims, the brave Count of Gascony, and others many. Roland came

CHARLES RECEIVES THE ENVOYS OF THE HEATHEN KING MARSILIUS.

too, followed by noble and valiant Oliver, and—lackaday he should have been there!—Roland's stepfather Ganelon, the felon and arch-traitor.

Charles opened that most disastrous council by repeating word for word King Marsilius's message.

"These are his promises," he concluded; "the question is—will he keep them?"

Before any one could say a word in reply, Roland started to his feet.

"Would you," he cried, "believe anything Marsilius says? 'T is seven full years since we came to Spain, and throughout the war he has shown himself faithless and treacherous. This is not the first time he sends you messengers with olive branches, and gifts, and promises. Once already fifteen of them came, and said exactly the same things. You took counsel with your Frenchmen, who, seeing you inclined to hear them, rashly approved your opinion: you trusted the Paynim, and sent him two of your Counts, Basil and Basan. He took their heads up there, in his mountains. No, no! Go on with the war as you have begun it; lead on to Saragossa, lay siege to it, though it last your lifetime; so will you best avenge them the felon slew."

The Emperor sat with bowed head, fingering his beard and twirling his moustache, and with no word replied to his nephew's speech, one way or the other. Silent, too, sat the Frenchmen, all except Ganelon. He rose, stood before Charles, and very haughtily began his discourse:

"You should not lend your ear to the words of fools. Nor to mine, nor to anybody's. Heed nothing but your own advantage. When King Marsilius sends you word that he is ready to become your vassal for all Spain and receive our faith, he who advises you to reject such offers cares little when or how we die. Pride should not sway your council. Heed not the fools; let wise men have their say."

Duke Naimes of Bavaria then stepped forward, old and wise, white with the snows of many winters; no more trusty vassal had the King.

Charlemagne Holds a Council

"To my mind," he said, "Count Ganelon spoke well. Marsilius is beaten in this war; you have taken all his castles, burned his cities, defeated his armies, and now he sues for mercy at your hands. It were unchristian to press him further, the more that he offers hostages for his sureties. You can do no better than send one of your barons to him, for there should be an end of this war."

Said the Frenchmen as one voice: "The Duke has spoken well!"

"Then, lords and barons, whom shall we send to Saragossa?" asked Charles.

"So it please you, my liege, I will go," said Duke Naimes.

"No!" replied Charles; "you are too wise a man. By my beard and whiskers, you shall not go so far from me. Sit down. No one asks anything more of you. Again I ask, my lords and barons, whom shall we send to Saragossa, to the Saracen King?"

Said Roland: "I don't see why I should not go."

"Certainly not," broke in Count Oliver;

"you are too rash and fiery. You would be sure to get into trouble. *I* had better go, if it please the King."

"Silence both!" cried Charles. "You shall not stir a foot in this matter, neither of you. By this white beard of mine, none of my twelve Peers shall go."

Silence fell on all. They sat quiet as chidden boys.

At last Turpin the Archbishop rose from his seat, and addressed Charles in a loud voice, as one having authority:

"Sir King, send none of your barons. In these seven years they have had more than their share of toil and dangers. Give *me* the glove and wand. I will go seek the Saracen and give him a piece of my mind."

But again the King angrily rebuked him:

"Go and sit down on that white rug! Not a word more, till you are addressed! French knights," he went on, "you must select a baron from my own land to be the bearer of my message to Marsilius."

"In that case," said Roland, "send

Ganelon, my stepfather; you will never find a fitter!"

"He is just the man!" cried all the knights. "If the King is willing, let him go!"

"Ganelon," said Charles "step nearer; from my hand receive the glove and wand. You are chosen unanimously—you heard it."

"Not so," retorts Ganelon; "this is all Roland's doing, and never in my life shall I love him more. Nor Oliver, because he is Roland's friend. Nor the twelve Peers, because they all love him. And here, before your eyes, Sir King, I challenge them all!"

"Curb your temper," Charles remarked, sternly. "It is my will; that is enough."

"I see I must go," said Ganelon; "but it will be with me as it was with Basil and his brother Basan: who that way goes, does not return. At least, Sir King, forget not that your sister is my wife. I have a son, Baldwin, the prettiest varlet you ever saw, and if he lives, he will grow into a bold warrior. I leave to him my lands and fiefs.¹ Take good care of him, I pray you. As for me, I shall never see him more."

"You are too tender-hearted," said Charles, coldly. "It is my will, and you must go."

Ganelon's anguish was pitiful to behold. He threw to the ground his cloak of sables and stood in his long silk tunic. His green eyes gleamed viciously, and his face was fierce. Yet even in this mood the Peers could not take their eyes off him, he was so handsome, with his tall and graceful figure, broad-hipped and supple.

"You fool!" he cried, addressing Roland, "what makes you rave like this against me? All the world knows I am your stepfather, and that is why you have

---

[1] A *fief* was land held from one superior in rank on certain conditions. The holder of the fief, or *vassal*, was bound to render certain services to his *liege lord*, the principal of which was the duty of attending him in war, with a fixed number of knights, men-at-arms, and horses, kept at his own expense. A vassal could in his turn bestow portions of the land on others, so they were of noble birth, on similar terms, and thus have vassals of his own. A king could be the vassal of another more powerful king. Such was the ladder of *feudal land tenure* which prevailed all through the Middle Ages, and which is known under the name of *the feudal system*.

a spite against me, and now doom me to this embassy. Have your way! But if, so God will, I come back alive, I will bring down on you such trouble and sorrow as will last you your lifetime."

"This is mere wild talk," replied Roland. "Everybody knows I take no account of threats. A wise and experienced man is needed for this embassy, and therefore I proposed you. Yet, if the King will let me, I shall be only too glad to go in your place."

"You shall not go in my place," retorted Ganelon; "you are not my vassal, and I am not your liege lord. Charles orders me for this service, and I will go. But once there, I know I shall do some mad thing or other, to give vent to my wrath."

At this, Roland laughed aloud, and this so incensed the Count, his heart was like to have split with rage. He was as one bereft of sense.

"I hate you!" he hissed, "for I owe it to you that this iniquitous choice has fallen on me."

Then, mastering his fury with a great

effort, he addressed Charles with proper respect:

"Great Emperor, you see me here before you, ready to do your will."

"Fair Sir Ganelon," said Charles, "listen: You shall, from me, say to Marsilius that he must become my vassal and receive holy baptism. Then will I give him half of Spain in fief; the other half will be for Roland. If Marsilius refuses these terms, I will go and lay siege to Saragossa, and he shall be made captive and bound by force; to Aix, my seat of empire, shall he be taken straight, by sentence there to die, in great sorrow and shame. Now take this letter with my seal attached, and with your own right hand give it to the Paynim King."

With the letter the Emperor gave the glove from his right hand to Ganelon, who wished himself a thousand miles away. As he put out his hand for it, the glove fell to the ground.

"O God! what may this portend?" the barons cried in alarm. "Surely from this embassy great harm will come to us."

"Time will show," said Ganelon. Then, to the Emperor: "Let me now crave my leave. Since I must go, there is no use in tarrying."

"Go," said the King, "for Jesus' honour and for mine."

Then with the right hand he blessed him and signed him with the cross, and gave him the wand and letter.

Without more delay Count Ganelon hied him to his quarters, and equipped himself with his handsomest armour. As he mounted his piebald charger, all the knights who stood around to see the last of him broke into tears and wailings:

"O baron, how hard your lot! You have been so long at court and were always held in such high honour by all! As for him who picked you out for this duty, Charlemagne himself shall be no protection to him. It was ill-advised of Cou— Such is his pleasure," replied w— erfrenchman; "and the man is not born us who could stand against him."

"The French are most valiant," went on the Saracen; "but your counts and bachelors? No, in sooth! For one to die is enough. As for you, return to sweet France, take my greeting to my wife, and to my father, and to Baldwin my son. Guard him well, and hold him for your lord."

With this he started on his way.

As he put out his hand for it glove fell to the ground.

"O God! what may this portend?" barons cried in alarm. "Surely from the embassy great harm will come to us."

III

GANELON'S EMBASSY AND TREASON

FOR some time Ganelon rode through an olive wood, till he joined the Saracen envoys, Blancandrin having ridden slowly on purpose to let him overtake them. The two soon fell to talking, each trying to sound the other, at which game, both being passing wily, they were well matched. Said the Saracen:

"A wonderful man is Charles! His conquests extend as far as the world. But what makes him so persistent in hunting us down here in our own land?"

"Such is his pleasure," replied the Frenchman; "and the man is not born who could stand against him."

"The French are most valiant," went on the Saracen; "but your counts and dukes serve their lord but ill in thus advising him. They are ruining him, and many with him."

"I know of none," replied Ganelon, "whom this blame would fit, save only Roland, and he will yet be brought to shame. His arrogance passes all bounds, and unless somebody puts him out of the world, we never shall have peace."

Said Blancandrin: "He must be very cruel and unjust. But who supports him in his arrogance?"

"The French," replied Ganelon. "They all love him and will never fail him. He is lavish with presents—steeds and mules, silken stuffs and armours. Even the Emperor he plies with gifts. Oh, he will yet conquer all the countries, even to the East."

Here the Saracen cast a sidelong critical glance at his companion: he thought him handsome, but detected the felon look in his eyes. Ganelon felt the glance, and a shiver ran through his frame. The Saracen must have been satisfied with what he saw, for he now spoke out freely.

"Listen!" he said; "would it not please you to take revenge on Roland? Well, then, by Mahomet! give him up to us. King Marsilius is courteously inclined, and all his wealth will be yours to choose from."

Ganelon heard, but said never a word. He rode on, with his chin on his breast.

By the time they reached Saragossa the two had become sworn allies and had agreed on the manner in which they would get rid of Roland. They dismounted under a yew, near where, under a great pine, on a throne all draped with Oriental silken stuffs, sat he who had till lately been King of all Spain. Twenty thousand Saracens stood around him, but not a word, not a breath was heard, so great was their anxiety to hear the news, when the messengers arrived.

Blancandrin approached Marsilius, leading Ganelon by the hand.

"All hail!" he began, "in the name of Mahomet and Apollo, whose holy law we follow! We delivered your messsage to Charles. He lifted both his hands to heaven, gave thanks to his God, and made no other answer. But he sent you one of his noblest barons, a most powerful man in France. From him you shall learn whether you are to have peace or no."

"Let him speak!" said Marsilius; "we will hear him."

Ganelon took just a moment to collect his spirits—for it required courage, unprotected as he was, to deliver such a message as Charles had given him. He did so, however, without omitting a word, and with unquaking voice. Marsilius was so infuriated when he had heard it to the end, that he would have hurled at the envoy a golden-shafted javelin which he held in his hand, had his arm not been seized. Ganelon saw the motion and drew his sword about two inches from the scabbard.

"As long as I have my sword," he cried, "it shall not be said that I died alone in foemen's land. Some of their best blood shall pay for mine."

The Saracens had hard work to prevent an affray; but at last they prevailed on the King to sit down again. The Frenchman, however, would not give up his sword; he held it fast by the golden hilt. The Paynims looked at him admiringly. "Truly," they said to each other, "this is a noble baron!" As for Ganelon, he once more approached the throne, and presented the Emperor's letter. Marsilius took it, still pale with suppressed rage. But his son was not to be appeased.

"Sir King!" he cried, "such speech as this man has uttered is death. Give him to me—and I will deal with him!"

Never, perhaps, was man nearer to his death than Ganelon at this instant. Yet he kept his countenance and, brandishing his sword, stood with his back against the trunk of the pine. Then Marsilius, to put an end to the tumult, rose and walked into his private gardens, taking with him only his son, his uncle and nearest friend, the Caliph, white-haired, crafty Blancandrin, and a few of his wisest and most trusted counsellors. Then Blancandrin announced his own particular tidings, which he would not tell before the general crowd.

"Send for the Frenchman," he said to the King; "he has pledged himself to us."

"Bring him yourself," commanded the King.

And the wily old Saracen led him in by the hand, and brought him before Marsilius. Then and there was hatched the infamous treason.

"Fair Sir," the King addressed him, "I was blinded by anger just now, when I offered to strike you. With these sables let me make amends: they are worth five hundred pounds in gold."

And with his own hands he clasped the precious mantle on the Frenchman's shoulders, who took them, nothing loth.

"I will not refuse a friendly gift," he said, "and may God requite you at His pleasure."

"Know then, Ganelon," began the King, "that I am minded to bear you much love. But what we speak here must remain a dead secret. Now, I would hear you tell of Charlemagne. Old, is he not? worn out and feeble? Why, he must be two hundred years old!¹ And through how many lands has he not dragged his body! How many hard knocks has he not received upon his buckler-shield! How many mighty kings has he not turned into beggars! Will he never be tired of all these wars?"

"No," replied Ganelon, "not he! No one that sees him and knows him well but will tell you that he is still a man in his prime. I never could find words that would do justice to his great worth and goodness. God has irradiated him with virtue. I would rather lose my life than my place among his barons. But he will never stop making war as long as his nephew lives. There is not Roland's match under the vault of heaven. His comrade Oliver, too, is a man of great prowess. The twelve Peers, beloved of Charles, lead the vanguard of twenty thousand knights. He is well guarded and need fear no living man."

"Fair Sir," Marsilius interrupted him,

[1] As a matter of history, Charles was only thirty-six in 778; he was born in 742.

"my people are the finest in the world, and I can still muster four hundred thousand knights to fight Charles and the French."

"And still you would not beat them," replied Ganelon, "but only lose great numbers of your men. Leave all this folly, and keep to the wiser course: give Charles enough money to make his men stare, and send the twenty hostages. He will then surely return to France, leaving behind a strong rear-guard for protection. Of that I am well assured Roland will be put in command, with brave and courteous Oliver. And then, believe me, the two Counts are as good as dead. This will be a great blow to Charles's pride, and he will never want to fight you more. He might better lose his right arm than Roland."

"But how shall I make sure of Roland?" anxiously asked the King.

"There will be twenty thousand French," replied the traitor. "Well, send a hundred thousand men. I do not say they will not suffer cruelly in the first onslaught; but let another follow, and a third—Roland cannot hold out forever."

Marsilius was so delighted that he clasped the Frenchman to his breast.

"What need of further talk?" he said. "Best make things safe and fast. Swear to me without more ado that you will compass his death. Swear that he will be in the rear-guard, and I will swear on my law, that, if I find him there, I will fight him."

Says Ganelon: "Your will be done!" and on the relics in the pommel of his sword swears to his treason. 'T is done—and he a felon forevermore!

Marsilius then, upon the book of Mahomet's law, swears his own oath.

And now the Paynim knights press round the Frenchman with offers of friendship and embraces, with presents too, each vying with the rest. One gives him a choice, richly mounted sword, another a helmet of finest workmanship. Even the Queen, fair Bramimonda, approaches him with gracious words:

"Fair Sir, I will love you greatly, for

my lord and all his knights hold you in high esteem. I want you to take this pair of armlets to your wife; they are all gold, amethysts, and rubies. Finer you will not find in Rome, and I doubt whether your Emperor ever had as fine."

"We are yours to command," he answers, and puts away the jewels in his boot.

Marsilius now called to his treasurer:

"Are the gifts for Charles in readiness?"

"They are," answered the man; "seven hundred camels laden with gold and silver, and twenty hostages, the noblest in the land."

Marsilius once more clasped Ganelon in his arms. Then holding him from him, with his hand upon his shoulder, and looking him sharply in the eye:

"Thou art a brave man," he said "and a wise. But, in the name of that law which you Christians hold sacred, I charge thee, never change thy mind about this, nor turn against us now. I will give largely of my wealth to thee: ten mule-loads now of finest gold of

Araby, and as much more every year. Now take the keys of this great city and give them to Charles with the treasure and the hostages. But be sure to have Roland placed in the rear-guard, that I may find him there."

"Methinks I am tarrying too long," says Ganelon, and, vaulting into the saddle, starts at once upon his return journey.

Charles was already on his way to France, and had reached Valtierra, one of the cities taken for him by Roland, and so thoroughly sacked and ruined that it remained a desert for full a hundred years after. There he staid encamped, to wait for news from Ganelon and the Spanish tribute; and there one morning, at dawn, his envoy found him.

It was a beautiful morning, with a cloudless sun. The Emperor had risen early, as was his wont, had heard matins and mass, and was sitting on the greensward, before his tent. Roland was there, and Oliver, and Duke Naimes, with many others. It was here that Ganelon presented himself and began his lying report, addressing the King:

"Greeting in the name of God!—Here I bring you the keys of Saragossa, and much treasure, with twenty hostages: place them under good guard. Valiant King Marsilius doth entreat you not to blame him, that he does not send you his uncle the Caliph. I have seen with my own eyes three hundred thousand men-at-arms, in full armour, embark upon the sea, under the Caliph's command. They were leaving the country, because they were not willed to accept the Christian faith. But they had not sailed four leagues from shore when they were overtaken by a gale and storm. They were all drowned and will be seen no more. Had the Caliph been alive, I should have brought him. As to the Paynim King, hold it for certain that, ere a month has passed, he will have followed you to your kingdom of France, there to receive the Christian law and become your humble vassal."

"Thanks be given to God!" said the

King. "Friend Ganelon, you have acquitted yourself well, and shall be well rewarded."

A thousand clarions then are sounded through the army. The French break camp, fold the tents, load the pack-horses and mules, and start on their way to the sweet land of France.

IV

THE REAR-GUARD—ROLAND'S DOOM

"THE war is over!" That was the thought uppermost in Charles's mind as he rode on blithely in the direction of his own sweet France. At the end of that first day's march, at eventide, Count Roland planted his banner on the top of a hill, while the French scattered over the country, pitching their tents wherever the fancy struck them. The Paynim host meanwhile rode in their rear and on their flanks, through wide valleys, in mailed hauberk or steel corslet, swords loose at the belt, helmets laced to the neck-piece of the armour, shields and lances all ready for action. They halted, four hundred thousand of them, in a wood for the night. Oh that the French could have seen through the intervening mountains!

The night was moonless and very dark. Charles slept, all unsuspecting. He had a dream: he thought he was riding through a narrow gorge in the mountains, holding in his hand his lance of hard ash-wood, when suddenly Count Ganelon wrenched it from him and broke it into splinters.

Charles did not wake. Then he had another dream. He was at his own city of Aix on the Rhine. A bear attacked him and bit his right arm so cruelly, the flesh was lacerated to the bone. Then, from the mountains of Ardenne, a leopard rushed on him and also attacked him most fiercely. But suddenly a greyhound came to the rescue from the palace in leaps and bounds, bit off the bear's right ear, and furiously assaulted the leopard. "A stupendous battle!" cried the French, and wondered who would win.

Still Charles slept on. The day broke clear and bright, a thousand clarions roused the army, and Charles, sitting on his charger, ready for the march, addressed his barons:

"Lords, ye see those narrow passes and defiles; whom shall I leave behind with the rear-guard, to hold them against possible pursuit?"

"Roland, my stepson!" Ganelon cried at once. "You have no braver baron, and our army will be safe under his guard."

Charles looked at him with displeasure.

"You are the Devil incarnate," he said. "What mortal rage possesses you? And who is to lead the vanguard before me?"

"Ogier of Denmark," Ganelon quickly replied; "he is most fit for the post."

When Roland heard that the choice had fallen on him he spoke in true knightly fashion:

"Sir stepfather, I must ever love you greatly and be beholden to you that you have named me for such honour. Charles, I vow, will not be a loser thereby. Nothing shall he miss if I know it—not a palfrey or charger, not a mule or a pack-horse, —but good blows will be exchanged first."

"You say true, and well I know it,"

said Ganelon, who saw that Roland was wroth with him, though he would not show it, and now attempted to propitiate him. But Roland ignored the clumsy flattery and spoke to Charles:

"Give me that bow you hold in your hand. No fear of my dropping it as Ganelon dropped your glove."

The Emperor sat still and thoughtful, with bowed head, twisting his beard, and ere he knew it there were tears in his eyes. As he gave Roland the bow he said:

"Surely you know, fair nephew, that I intend to leave with you half my army."

"Never in the world!" broke in the Count. "Heaven confound me if I shame my blood! I will take twenty thousand French knights, not a man more. As for you, go your ways in all peace of mind: you need fear no man so long as I am alive."

Count Roland now goes to his tent to arm himself. He dons his hauberk of shining mail, laces his helmet to his armour, girds on his own good sword, Durendal of the golden hilt, and hangs on his neck by a broad baldrick his shield all flower-painted; of all his steeds he mounts his favourite, Veillantif. In his right hand he takes his lance with the white pennon, of which the golden fringe falls down to the hilt of his sword. Around him range themselves his comrade Oliver, Gerin, and Gerier, the valiant brothers; Otho and Berenger, and Duke Samson, and sundry more of Charles's most loved companions. "By my life! I too will stay with you," says Turpin, the warlike Archbishop of Rheims. Between them they select twenty thousand knights.

That same day the army entered the pass of Roncevaux—a place to shudder at, so high are the mountains, so deep and dark the valleys, so narrow and rugged the gorge, overtopped on both sides with dizzy black rocks. The tramp of the horses was heard for miles around. There was something gloomy and depressing about the place, and there was not one but gave way to the mysterious influence. They fell to thinking of their own domains, their noble wives, and fair young daughters, and all felt the melting mood upon them. But the most sorrowful of all was Charles, for he was leaving his nephew in this dreadful pass. The twelve Peers with their twenty thousand men entered it along with the main body, but did not come out at the same time, for were they not to stay behind, to protect the others that were to go before, all the way home? Therefore was it that Charles wept and hid his face in the folds of his mantle.

"What thought weighs on you so heavily?" asked old Duke Naimes, who rode nearest to the King.

"You wrong me by asking," replied Charles. "My heart is so full of grief, I must weep. Ganelon will be the ruin of France. Last night, in a dream sent by my guardian angel, I saw him break my lance between my own hands,—this same Ganelon who made me put my nephew in command of the rear-guard. And now I have left Roland in this foreign land! Oh! if I lose him—my God! I shall never find his like."

The great Emperor let his tears flow

freely; all looked on him with pity, and all were moved with a strange, boding fear for Roland. Ganelon saw it all, and, knowing what was coming, kept his counsel—for was he not paid to keep it?

Marsilius, in the meantime, had summoned all his Paynim nobles; four hundred thousand came together in three days,—and the drum was heard in all the streets of Saragossa. On the top of the city's highest tower the statue of Mahomet was set up for all to pray to and adore.[1] Then they rode in furious haste across country, over mounts and vales, till they saw from afar the banners of the French—the rear-guard with the Peers! They halted and mustered their forces in battle array.

King Marsilius's nephew rode out in front of the ranks and declared his intention of engaging Roland himself in single combat, asking as the one boon he craved,

---

[1] Another glaring incongruity: the Mussulmans are forbidden by Mahomet's law to counterfeit the human form either in painting or sculpture. This prohibition was prompted by excessive fear of a possible leaning towards idolatry.

The Rear-Guard

that the Christian chief be left to his prowess alone. At the same time he called on the King to choose eleven knights who should, with him, be the match of the twelve French Peers. Eleven champions at once eagerly responded. Thus was formed the company of the twelve Saracen Peers. Each strove to outbrag all the others in rehearsing their future exploits, so that, to hear them, one marvelled much they did not ride forth for Roncevaux alone. But they took a hundred thousand Saracens with them, leaving three times as many, to rescue or support them, since they well knew with whom they had to deal and did not expect to win at the first onslaught. They armed themselves most carefully in a wood of ancient firs, and leaving their pack-horses and the mules on which they were wont to travel for greater ease, mounted their richly caparisoned chargers and rode on in orderly serried ranks.

The noise of their starting and the shrill blasts of their clarions were heard by the French, for the day was clear and still, and every sound went far.

"Sir comrade," Oliver said to his friend, "meseems we are like to do battle soon with the Saracens."

"God grant it!" he replied; "that is what we are here for. It is every good vassal's duty to suffer any hardship for his liege, be it cold or heat, to give and take hard knocks in his service, and not spare his own skin. We must see to it that our names be not shamed in song, and I for one will not give a bad example."

PART SECOND

ROLAND'S DEATH

I

BEFORE THE BATTLE

OLIVER climbed upon a hill from which he could see far down the valley on the Spanish side, and beheld the whole Paynim army spread out below. He called Roland to his side.

"I knew," he said, "that noise came from the Spanish side. See how all those hauberks gleam! How the helmets flash! Our Frenchmen have some hard work before them. It is all Ganelon's doing, the felon! It was he who talked the Emperor into putting us on this duty."

"Silence, Oliver!" Roland rebuked him.

"Remember, he is my mother's lord—not a word against him!"

For a long time Oliver stood, viewing the Saracen host, but the great motley multitude was confusing to the eye; so he made his way down to his friends and told them what he had seen.

"There are surely a hundred thousand of them," he concluded; "we shall have a battle such as was never seen. Stand fast, and God give you strength!"

They answered him with enthusiastic shouts.

Said thoughtful Oliver:

"The enemy are in great force, and we are very few. Friend Roland, sound your Olifant[1]: Charles will hear it and return."

"Do you take me for a fool?" Roland retorted angrily. "I should be the laughing-stock of France. No! my good sword, my Durendal, will strike hard; so will all our men. The heathens will find they were ill-inspired to come to these de-

---

[1] "Olifant"—Roland's ivory horn. Ivory was called "olifant" (from "elephant").

files: they are doomed, every one, I dare be sworn."

"Friend Roland, sound your Olifant!" Oliver repeated, with greater insistence. "Charles will hear it and will return with the main army to our aid."

"God forbid," Roland again replied, "that I should bring shame upon my kin and upon my country! No! my Durendal and I will fight it out—you will see the blade up to its golden hilt in blood. The Paynims, I repeat, in coming here signed their own death-warrant."

"Friend Roland, sound your Olifant," Oliver entreated for the third time,— and for the third time, and more angrily, Roland refused, on the plea of shame to himself and dishonour to France.

"I cannot see where would be the dishonour," persisted Oliver, "since they are so many and we so few."

But Roland's bravery had some of the quality of stubbornness in it, and nothing in the world could now have moved him to take his comrade's wise advice. And while they were thus bandying words, the

Saracens had been riding on fast and furious.

"See, Roland, see!" cried Oliver; "they are upon us, and Charles now is very far. Ah! you would not sound your Olifant! Had you done so, the King would soon be here and we would not be in so much danger. Whatever betide, they will not be to blame. Look at our ranks here in the pass; many are going to this battle who will never see another."

"Speak not so idly!" Roland broke in, "cursed be he that carries a faint heart this day! We will hold our own right valiantly. Let us strike the first blow, not wait to be attacked."

With the approach of battle, he felt light of heart and fierce as any lion or leopard; he turned his horse and addressed his friend and their small army in a short, inspiring speech:

"I pray thee, comrade, speak not like that again. Here we are, twenty thousand of us, set apart by Charles himself, and not a faint heart among us, as he knows well. Make good use of thy lance, friend Oliver, as I will not spare Durendal, my good sword given me by the King. And if I die, whoever has it after me will say 'This was a noble vassal's sword.'"

Archbishop Turpin now rode up the hill and took a look at the enemy; then, turning to the French, he delivered to them the following sermon:

"Lords and barons! Charles has left us here: he is our king and we should be ever ready to die for him. Christendom is in peril—stand by it! It is certain that you will have a battle, for here are the Saracens before your eyes. Then strike your breasts, confess your sins, and commend yourselves unto God's mercy. For the good of your souls I will assoilzie you, and if you die, you will all be martyrs: your places are waiting for you in God's great Paradise."

At the words all the knights dismount and humbly kneel upon the ground. The Archbishop extends his arm, blesses them in the name of God, and concludes:

"And be your penance to strike Paynims!"

It was with lightened hearts the knights rose from their knees, freed of their load of sin, at peace with God and blest, and again mounted their fleet chargers, ready and eager for battle. Roland called Oliver to him, perhaps regretting his burst of temper.

"Comrade," he said, "you were right in saying that it was Ganelon who betrayed us. He will have traded us for a goodly sum in gold and silver. As for Marsilius, who bought us, our swords shall clinch the bargain he struck with the traitor."

As Roland rode into the pass on his good steed Veillantif, in his richest armour, the golden fringe from his white pennon drooping along the shaft of his lance down to his hand, with open, smiling countenance, he looked the very ideal of a noble knight; the French looked on him with loving pride and greeted him with the cry "Hail to our champion!" Oliver rode but a step behind. Roland's glance was

ARCHBISHOP TURPIN BLESSES THE FRENCH ARMY LEFT AT RONCEVAUX.

dark and fierce as he cast it on the Saracens, gentle and modest as his eye rested on his own people, and he halted for a courteous word:

"Lords and barons, walk your horses; save yourselves and them. These heathens, in sooth, have come a long way for what they will get. And think what glorious booty there will be for us! No King of France ever gathered richer."

But Oliver was not to be cheered or distracted from his gloomy forebodings.

"I don't care to talk," he said, brusquely. "You would not sound your horn; Charles's help is sorely needed. Certainly, whatever befall us, he will not be to blame, nor those who are with him, since they know not a word of this. Now all that is left us is to ride hard, and strike hard, and die hard. For God's sake, think of only these two things: to give and to take hard blows. And let us not forget Charles's own battle-cry."

"Mountjoy! Mountjoy!" the French shout as one man, and, spurring on their steeds, increase their pace, and—

for what else could they do?—charge the foe.

Thus French and Saracens came to blows.

II

THE BATTLE

MARSILIUS'S young nephew rode in front of the Paynim host, to show off his splendid armour and his brave and handsome steed, at the same time hurling defiance and abuse at the French, and taunting them with their plight:

"Ye foolish French, now will ye be forced to fight. They who should have defended you have betrayed you. Your Emperor must be demented to leave you here in this narrow pass. Here France shall forfeit her glorious name, and Charles lose what is to him as the right arm of his body. There will at last be rest for Spain!"

Roland heard the words, and, frantic with grief and anger, charged the speaker with such fury that, at one stroke of his lance, he shattered the Saracen's shield, pierced through his mailed hauberk and through the bones of his breast till it broke the backbone, and the youth's soul left his body as it swayed in the saddle and dropped on the ground, the first dead of that great day, while Roland replied to his taunts:

"Go! thou wretch, thou caitiff! and know that Charles never loved traitor or treason. He left us here because such are the needs of war, and France never shall forfeit her glorious name through us."

Another Paynim chief of repute, King Marsilius's own brother, was hard by—a man of giant stature and of most ferocious aspect. Rage seized him as he saw his nephew fall, and he rushed from the front rank, shouting insults and threats. He was met by Oliver, whose lance transfixed him with such violence that the folds of the pennon were forced into the wound.

"Reprobate! I care not for thy threats," he cried, looking down on the vast size of the man, as he lay lifeless at his feet.

"At them, ye French! we will beat them yet!"

And, shouting "Mountjoy!" Charles's own battle-cry, he rushed on the foe.

Archbishop Turpin now found himself confronted by one of Marsilius's vassal kings, who was urging on his men:

"On! on! we can easily hold the field alone—there are so few of them! Not one shall escape; Charles is powerless to help, and nothing can stave off their doom!"

The Archbishop gave his horse the spurs and was upon the Saracen before he had done speaking: at that moment it seemed to him there was not a man under the sun whom he hated as he hated this foul-mouthed heathen. The next instant he had him off his horse, dead.

"Thou didst lie in thy throat, thou dastardly pagan! Charles, our lord, is still our hope and stay, and if we are few, there are still enough of us to keep you busy here a while. At them, ye French! We had the first stroke, thank God!"

And he too shouts "Mountjoy!" and gallops across the narrow field.

But the battle does not, for some time yet, become general. The more prominent warriors on each side pick out adversaries on the other, and the engagement is not so much a battle as a number of single combats fought at the same time at different points. The advantage, so far, is decidedly on the side of the French, and the twelve Peers, with even more than their habitual prowess, have each fought and killed his man—all with the lance alone, for it is early in the day, and swords are not drawn until the lances give out.

The first sword unsheathed was Roland's Durendal: it cut a Saracen knight in twain down to his horse and through the saddle, though it was plated with gold, and deep down into the horse's back. After this Durendal might be seen flashing at all points of the field as Roland swung it round and round, flinging bodies on bodies in heaps, his horse standing and wading in running blood, himself crimson from head to foot. The twelve Peers kept closest to him—but none of the knights was remiss; the battle-cry "Mountjoy! Mountjoy!" rang lustily on every side, the Archbishop's voice loud above the rest. Oliver alone still plied the lance, until it snapped in his fist.

"How now, comrade!" cried Roland, "what would you with a stick in such a battle? Good steel is needed here. Where is your sword, with the hilt of gold and the pommel of pure crystal?"

"Faith! I had no time to draw it," he replied; "I was too busy striking."

As day advances the battle rages more and more madly. Oliver and Roland, the Archbishop and the Peers, with all their prowess, can hardly be said to excel the other knights. All are desperate; all fight as those who know that never again shall they see mothers, or wives, or friends, or any of them that wait for them beyond the passes.

That same morning of the great battle in the fatal pass of Roncevaux, a tremendous storm swept over the whole of France,—a storm the like of which no man then alive had ever seen. The rain and hail that fell were heavy beyond all measure, the gale and thunder were terrific beyond words, the lightning struck oft and hard, and the earth was felt to quake. From St. Michael's Mount on the coast of Normandy to Cologne on the Rhine, there were few houses of which the roofs or walls were whole. From noon to the hour of vespers dense darkness enwrapped the world as at the dead of night, and no light was seen but that of the lightnings cleaving the blackness. Men were stunned with fear at such portents and many said "This is the end of time and of all things." Alas, no: it was only nature mourning for Roland's great agony and inevitable death, and that of so many brave men with him.

For the battle now was raging horribly, most deadly—the second, decisive test.

The morning's engagement had ended favourably for the French. The Saracens had fled, panic-stricken, in disorder, leaving the field strewed with broken lances, tattered pennons, shining hauberks and corslets, and most of their men stretched on the blood-soaked grass. But even flight could not save the survivors: the pursuit was so hot that all fell as they fled, and only one—the vassal King Margaris—escaped alive, though with four gaping wounds, broken lance, shattered shield, mail shirt torn and bedraggled, sword dulled, hacked, and bloody. In this plight, fainting, fordone, he fell to the ground at Marsilius's feet.

"To horse! to horse!" he gasped. "You will find the French tired out with killing and pursuing. Half of them are dead; the other half are mostly wounded, and all exhausted. Their arms, too, are mostly broken or gone, and they can get no others. You will find it easy work now to avenge us—they are just ripe for slaughter."

Soon after there was a great shout through the French host:

"Help, help, ye Peers! Here is Marsilius himself with a hundred thousand more!"

Roland, Oliver, and almost all the knights had dismounted to take breath and a brief respite. The Archbishop solemnly addressed them:

"Men of God! be brave and undaunted in this your hour of glory! This is the day when the crown will be placed on your brow by angel hands, and Paradise will open wide to receive you."

There was a moment of pity and grief uncontrollable; the knights embraced and wept over one another with the tenderness of great friendship, and exchanged farewell kisses. But Roland cried, "To horse, now, to horse!" and in an instant all were in the saddle.

King Marsilius came on, keeping the middle of the valley, with his forces divided into twenty columns. The gold and precious stones of the helmets twinkled in the sun, so did the lances with their pennons, the burnished shields, and shining hauberks. Seven thousand clarions sound the charge.

"Oliver, my comrade, my brother!" cried Roland, "that traitor Ganelon has sworn our death, it is too evident. But our Emperor will surely take direst vengeance on him. As for us, nothing is left us but to fight and bear ourselves so that no jeering rhymes are made in France about us."

Archbishop Turpin, before he leads the charge with Roland, Oliver, and the Peers, takes time for a last exhortation:

"Let not any regretful thought now unman you, barons! Nothing can be more certain than that this day we die: let us then die fighting, nor yield one foot of ground. Not one of us will be alive to-morrow. But one thing I can promise you with certainty as great: it is that Paradise will open wide for you. To-morrow ye shall all be seated with the saints."

These words inspire the French with courage more than human, and they spur their chargers on, to the one general cry, "Mountjoy!"

Marsilius, meanwhile, was also addressing his men.

"Count Roland," he said, "is a man of passing great prowess; to conquer him will be no easy thing; even two battles may not suffice. Well, he shall have a third. But this day shall see Charles shorn of half his boasted greatness and France brought to shame."

He stationed himself on the brow of a rocky height, while his general, carrying the royal, gold-embroidered banner, galloped at full speed down into the valley and bore down upon the French, from whose ranks burst a loud curse against the traitor who had sold them. But the Archbishop would not let profane feelings prevail at this dread hour, and recalled them to holier thoughts:

"Good knights," he cried, "this is the day of your greatest honour, when God himself will crown you, and place you in Paradise among the elect, in his glory, where ye shall rest bedded on flowers of Eden. But never shall coward enter there."

"We will acquit ourselves so as not to shame you," they shouted; "we will die, but will not fail you, nor be felons to God!"

And now the battle is on in earnest.

Such a battle! Death rides the field from end to end. The narrow valley closes both armies in, giving them no room to spread and move in, so that the wounded and the dead, riders and steeds, fall and lie in heaps many high, and are trampled again and again, as the battle rages close by them—nay upon them. Not so much a battle as blind slaughtering. Forgotten all rules of chivalry, all customs of war; swords pierce and cut at random: heads, and arms, and legs fly right and left; skulls are cleft to the chin and neck, through helmet, visor, and nose-guard; armour is cut and shattered; mail broken and torn. The fury of the French is such that, though not half of them are left, they bid fair once more to rout the Saracens—the third Paynim host. Archbishop Turpin seems to be at all points at once; never did mass-chanting priest perform such marvels of martial prowess. Roland, Oliver, and the Peers seem to the pagans bloody spirits of carnage, not men. Each comrade whom they see fall seems to increase tenfold, not their fury alone, but their strength and valour. But even as they ply the deadly work, grief gnaws at their hearts, and they think with anguish, "O God, how our friends fall!" And still they pursue the Saracens, through blood that reaches to their horses' bellies. Their swords of fine steel are broken or blunted; their lances have long been shattered; they have no weapons left; they fight with the stumps, they break heads with their horns, their clarions, till the Paynims loudly curse the day they came to the fateful pass of Roncevaux.

There are still three hundred swords available, and they work to such good purpose that the Saracens fly before them, nor ever stop till they reach the spot whence Marsilius watches the battle, black fury at his heart, and cry to him for aid. Among those swords, the best in the French host, there is none that compares with Roland's noble Durendal, unless it be Oliver's sword. For an instant Roland pauses and watches his friend, and a wave of great tenderness sweeps over his heart.

STEEL HELMET WITH NOSE-GUARD (NASEL).

(*From Seals, XIIth Century.*)

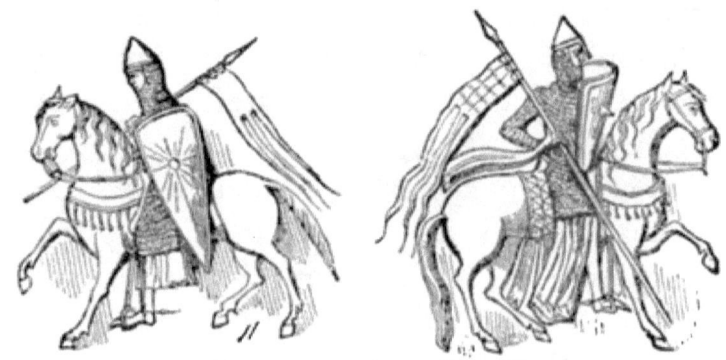

HAUBERKS, WORN OVER TUNICS, AND PENNANTS.

(*From Seals, XIIth Century.*)

"Ah, noble Count," he calls to him, "so loyal and so brave, this day our friendship must end,—this is the day of our most sorrowful parting. Never more shall our Emperor see either of us; never shall there have been such mourning in the sweet land of France. Not a Frenchman but will pray for us, not an abbey or monastery but there will be masses said for our souls, which will then already be in Paradise."

Oliver heard his comrade's words, and pushed on to his side, forcing his way through the fighting multitude.

"Let us keep together!" they said. "If so it please God, we will not die apart."

From this moment these two and the Archbishop managed not to let themselves be separated by any accident of the battle. The number of those they killed is recorded in charters and in song —they are said to have been over four thousand. The first four onslaughts were favourable to the French, but the fifth was fatal: all the knights perished then, save only sixty. God spared no more. But these sixty were to sell their lives at a price which the Paynims were very loth to pay.

III

THE OLIFANT

ROLAND, seeing the great number of their slain friends, said to Oliver:

"Dear comrade, is it not a pitiful sight —these many loyal vassals stretched lifeless on the ground? Ah, surely we may mourn for our fair France, widowed of so many doughty barons. Oh, why is not our friend the King here with us, to aid and save us! Oliver, my brother, what can we do to convey to him the evil tidings?"

"Nay, I see no way," quoth Oliver. "But one thing I know: better death than dishonour."

"I will blow my horn," said Roland, "my Olifant. Charles will hear it, for he has only just passed out of the defile, and he will return in haste, I will be sworn."

"That were great shame," retorted Oliver; "all your kin would blush for you, and the dishonour would cling to them through life. When I advised it, you would not. Had you taken my advice then, the Emperor would be here now, and we should not be in such sorry plight. By my beard, if ever I see again my gentle sister Aude, you shall never take her to your home as your bride."

"Why will you be so wroth with me?" said Roland sadly.

"Because this is your doing" Oliver replied. "Courage is one thing, reckless rashness is another, and there should be measure in all things. It is through your thoughtless foolhardiness so many Frenchmen had to die, and we ourselves can never more serve the Emperor. Had you listened to me, he would be here; the battle should now be won and done, Marsilius either dead or captive. Ah, Roland, your ill-timed bravery will be our ruin; your death will not save France from dishonour. Alas that this should be the end of our most loyal friendship! For long ere night we shall be parted most cruelly."

His voice broke, and they wept and sighed most piteously, each for the other.

The Archbishop, hearing Oliver's chiding, hastened to their side.

"Sir Roland and you, Sir Oliver, I beseech you," he cried, "quarrel not at such a time. For see—we are doomed. Your horn cannot save us; Charles is far by this time and would come too late. Still, my advice is that you blow it. If too late to save, the King will be in time to avenge us, and at least the Paynims will not return homeward triumphant. Our countrymen will dismount and find us, even though dead and hacked to pieces; they will lay our mangled remains in rough-hewn biers, which their own steeds shall bear out of these dreadful mountains, back to our own sweet land of France, and there we shall be laid to rest in churches and cloisters. At least our bodies shall not be devoured by dogs, wild boars, and wolves. Sound, then, your Olifant, I say."

"And you say well," replied Roland.

Forthwith, setting the horn to his lips, he sounded on it a blast, full and long, with all his gathered breath. So powerful was the blast that Charles heard it, doubled by the echo beyond the mountains, some thirty leagues away. Nor Charles alone; the whole army heard, and marvelled.

"Our men are fighting," said the King. But Ganelon quickly cut him short:

"Did anyone but you say such a thing, he would be called a liar."

Once again, with anguish and great pain, Roland sounded his Olifant. The crimson blood spurted from his mouth with the strain. But the blast went far beyond the pass, where the French army was riding leisurely along. Charles heard it, and Duke Naimes, and all stopped to listen. And again the King said:

"That was Roland's horn. He never would sound it, were he not hard pressed in battle."

"There is no battle," Ganelon insisted peevishly. "You are old, your locks are

ROLAND'S DEATH-BLAST ON THE "OLIFANT."

scant and white, and you speak the words of a child. You know full well Roland's exceeding pride—Roland the strong, the great, the marvellous! Truly, it is a wonder that God tolerates him so long. For a hare he will blow his horn all day. Surely, he is having some fun with the Peers. Besides, who would dare attack him? Ride on, I say. Why should you halt? The country before us is vast, and the road is long."

A third time Roland sounds his Olifant. His mouth is all bloody, a blood-vessel bursts in his temple with the desperate strain. All hear it this time—there is no room for doubt.

"That horn has a tremendous force!" said the King.

"'T is Roland!" cried Duke Naimes; "Roland in the throes of death! On my soul, there is a battle, and somebody has betrayed him—and that somebody is he who is dissembling and trying to keep you here. Arm you, Sir King! Call out your battle-cry! Haste to the rescue, for 't is Roland's plaint you hear."

At the Emperor's word of command, all the horns and clarions sound at once; the barons arm themselves in haste, mount their fleetest chargers and spur them back through the gorges they have just passed; one thought is in everyone's mind, on everyone's lips: "If only we find Roland alive!"

Too late, alas! Too late!

From the moment that Charles knew in his heart that treason was abroad, he also knew with absolute certainty who was the traitor. He ordered Ganelon to be seized and bound, and gave him in charge to his chief cook.

"Guard me that man well," he said to him; "he is the traitor who has sold me and my house."

The cook took Ganelon to his quarters and set a hundred of his fellows at him. They belaboured him with fists and sticks and switches, pulled the hairs of his head and beard, and at last chained him by the neck as they would a bear, and flung him, like a bale of goods, across a pack-horse's back. And so they kept him all through that mad ride and after, until they gave him up to Charles for judgment.

Ah me, what a ride was that! Between those mountains, so high, precipitous, so darkly frowning, through those deep gorges, with the headlong, roaring torrents! Charles had ordered all the horns and trumpets, in front and rear, to sound unceasingly, to answer Roland's horn and give notice of the host's approach. Charles rode harder than many a younger man, silent, with set face, his heart swelling with grief and rage. Behind him rode all the French, silent too with suppressed feeling; tears rained unchecked down many a deep-lined cheek, and here and there a sob was heard; and all were praying in their hearts as they would never pray again, that God would but keep Roland alive until they came, and they would wrest him from the very jaws of death. On, on they rode, with not a minute's halt, not an instant's slackening of the reins.

Too late, alas! Too late!

IV

OLIVER'S DEATH

SIXTY men! To that handful is reduced the rear-guard under Roland's command. As he looks at them, and at all the dead that cover the ground and the slopes wherever they were not too steep to fight, he feels that instant death were the most welcome boon. But he remembers that among these sixty are several of the Peers and of Charles's bravest and best-loved knights, and knows that, if he is killed, not one of them will survive. So far, by a happy chance little short of a miracle, he has escaped without a single wound. Only he begins to feel a mortal weariness steal over him, and at times his limbs feel numb. He weeps, the noble knight, as he looks upon so many comrades slain.

"Barons, my brethren," he says in gentlest accents, "may God be merciful to your souls! May he grant you all a place in Heaven, and give you rest on flowers of Paradise! Better, more loyal vassals, I never saw. It is through me you had to die—I see it now—and I was powerless to help, to save! God help you, He who never failed any man! Oliver, my brother Oliver, stay by me. If I am not killed here by the enemy, I shall die of a broken heart. Come, comrade! let us back to our work—kill! kill! and no quarter!"

As the friends rushed back into the fray, the Archbishop cheered on their sixty followers with a few approving and encouraging words:

"This is as it should be! This is how a true knight should bear himself, who has good arms and a good horse. Else were he good only to be made a cloistered monk, and spend his life praying for our sins."

When a man knows he can expect no quarter, he is unconquerable in battle. The French, therefore, went into this last fray fierce as lions. This time Marsilius himself led the onslaught and showed himself a right royal champion; several of the Peers fell at his hand, but Roland was upon him in a twinkling, and, brandishing Durendal, struck off his right hand at the wrist. The panic was so great among the Saracens when they saw their King disabled that, as he turned bridle, they followed at full speed and never looked behind.

But, lack-a-day! what good, at this late hour, was even such a victory? Marsilius fled, it is true, but there was his uncle, the Caliph, bringing in fresh troops—the negro contingent from Ethiopia, as many as fifty thousand.

When Roland saw the accursed throng, blacker than ink, with nothing white about them but their rows of teeth, he called his knights to strike, strike as long as their swords held out, for the honour of France —" For," said he, " when Charles our lord comes to this field of death, and finds fifteen Saracens lying dead by each one of us, he cannot but bless us in his heart."

Roland's feeling that this was the last, the fatal shock, did not deceive him, for one of the first killed by the blacks was Oliver, whom their leader, the Caliph himself, transfixed through the body with his lance, breaking through the mail-work of the hauberk. Yet death was not immediate, and Oliver still had the strength to turn on his slayer and cleave his head to the teeth with one tremendous blow of his sword—that sword which had no match but Durendal alone.

"Go, accursed heathen!" he cried. "I will not say that Charles has not lost much; but thou certainly shalt not boast, to thy wife or any other dame in the land of thy birth, of any damage thou mayest have done him, in slaying either me or any other of his knights."

Then suddenly his strength gave way, and with a last effort he shouted, "Roland! Roland! help! hither, to me!"

When Roland looked in his friend's

face, and saw it discoloured, livid, and saw the blood streaming down his body to the earth, the shock was too great; and with a cry of despair, he nearly lost consciousness, sitting on his horse.

Oliver, meanwhile, had lost so much blood that his sight became blurred, and he could not have known any man, even at his very side. Thus, unconsciously turning his horse, he stumbled against his friend and, knowing him not, from sheer instinct, struck at his golden helmet and cleft it down to the nose-guard, but, by great good fortune, the sword did not cut the skull. Roland looked at him, bewildered, then, seeing how it was, spoke to him sadly and lovingly:

"Comrade mine, did you do that on purpose? I am Roland, who loves you as his soul. You did not challenge me, that I know?"

"I hear you," replied Oliver, "I hear your voice, but cannot see you. God guard you, friend. Was it you I struck? Forgive me!"

"You did not hurt me," said Roland;

STATUES OF ROLAND AND OLIVER IN THE PORTALS OF THE
CATHEDRAL AT VERONA, IN NORTHERN ITALY
(XIIth CENTURY).

"I forgive you, freely, here and before God."

They bent towards each other and most lovingly embraced.

Oliver felt the anguish of coming death, he could not see or hear; so softly glided from the saddle and lay him down on the ground. Loudly he spoke his "*Mea culpa*" and, folding his hands, extended them towards heaven, praying God to bless Charles, sweet France, and his comrade Roland above all men. Then his heart stood still, his head fell back, and he lay stretched on the ground, at rest.

When Roland saw that all was over, that his heart's friend was dead beyond recall, he could not at first control his grief, but broke into tears and sobs.

"My comrade! my brother!" he exclaimed, "that thy bravery should have brought thee to this! So many years, so many days have we lived together, and never didst thou do me harm, or I to thee. Now thou art dead, it is pain to me to live."

Long did Roland mourn over his friend.

And when he recovered himself and looked around him, he saw that all the French were dead, save only two: the Archbishop and one Count Gautier, who had just descended from a mountain, which he had held against the Saracens till all his companions were killed. He was faint with many wounds and only wanted to die by the side of friends. Roland cut in strips his long silken tunic, to bind up his hurts as best he could, and the next moment already the Paynims were upon them from all sides at once. But when they saw these three, shoulder to shoulder, at bay, ready for the last desperate fight, no longer for life, but only honour, they dared not approach them, but hurled at them, from a safe distance, lances, spears, arrows, javelins. Gautier, already exhausted, fell from the first; next the Archbishop was hit by four lances, and, his horse being killed under him, was thrown to the ground. But he was instantly on his feet again, and ran towards Roland, shouting:

"I am not conquered yet. So long as

a brave warrior has breath, he does not give up the fight."

Charles said later that where Turpin was found, four hundred Paynims were lying around him, some wounded, some cut in two, and some headless.

Roland, though still unscathed, was very nearly at the end of his strength. His body burned in an intolerable fever, his head pained him almost to distraction, and his one conscious thought was now "Is Charles coming?" He took his horn and drew from it one last feeble blast. But, feeble as it was, the Emperor, who was already very near, heard it and halted.

"Barons," he said, "things are going ill. My nephew Roland is lost to us. From the sound of his horn I know he is in mortal straits. If you would be in time, press on, spur your steeds. And sound all the trumpets we have in the host!"

Then was heard the blare of sixty thousand trumpets, so loud that the mountains caught up the sound and the valleys rang with it. The Paynims heard, and never in their lives were they less inclined to laugh! "It is Charles!" they said each to other, and "Charles is coming!" ran through their ranks from front to rear. "If Roland survives, the war will begin all over again, and Spain is lost to us!"

Then four hundred of the bravest Saracen warriors formed a flying squadron and rushed to where Roland held his ground doggedly with Turpin, the Archbishop. But just at that moment the trumpets sounded again nearer and nearer,—and the Saracens turned bridle and galloped away, but halted at a distance, and sent another shower of lances, arrows, and javelins, at the two champions. Still Roland was untouched, but his charger, his beloved Veillantif, fell dead under him. Then they fled on, leaving him alone with his one companion, and afoot.

"Roland," they said, "still has the best of us. For he is alive and the Emperor is coming—hear his clarions! To wait for him were death. So many noble kings are humbled at his feet, it is not Marsilius who ever could stand against him."

V

THE ARCHBISHOP'S LAST BLESSING

THE two friends are left alone at last and unmolested. The Paynims have taken the road to Spain and do not look back any more. Then Roland hastens to where the Archbishop lies, fordone and nearly dead, and tends him with gentle hand. He unlaces his golden helmet, strips off his light mail-shirt, tears up his tunic into strips to bind up the broad gashes on his body, then tenderly takes him in his arms and very gently lays him on a green grassy spot. Having thus given him as much ease as is possible in their forlorn plight, he speaks to him of something which sorely oppresses his heart:

"Noble friend! give me leave to beg of

you a boon. Our comrades, they whom we so loved, are all dead, but we should not leave them thus uncared for. I will go and look them up one by one; I will bring them here, and lay them in a row before you."

"Go," said the Archbishop, "and return promptly. Thank Heaven, the field is ours!"

Roland went, all alone, from end to end of the battle-field; he searched the valley and the mountainside, and one by one he found his comrades. He called each of them by name, and one after another he carried the ten Peers to where Turpin lay,—at his feet he laid them down reverently, in a row. The Archbishop could not but weep at the piteous sight, and raising his hand, gave them his pastoral blessing, saying:

"Good lords, may God, who brought you here to die, take all your souls and rest them in Paradise amid holy flowers. My own hour is come—I will not see again our great Emperor."

But Roland's pious task was not yet

done. Once more he returned and searched the valley, until, under a pine, he found the body of his comrade Oliver. Lovingly he raised him in his arms, and holding him tightly clasped against his breast, he made his way, tottering and stumbling with great weariness, back to the Archbishop. There, by the side of the other Peers, he laid him on a shield, to receive the prelate's blessing and absolution.

Long did Roland stand and gaze upon the dead Peers and his dear comrade, until, overcome with tenderness, he burst into tears and fell senseless by the side of him whom he had loved in life and now loved and mourned in death. The Archbishop was moved with such exceeding grief at the sight that, for one brief moment, he forgot his own deadly hurts, and seizing on the Olifant, dragged himself painfully, on hands and feet, towards a little spring which bubbled from a rock near by, thinking to gather in the horn a little of the icy-cold water to revive his friend. He almost reached it, but not quite—his last strength gave way from the great loss of blood; he fell upon his face, in death's last agony.

Thus Roland found him, when he recovered from his swoon and, looking to the right and to the left, nor seeing him near, went in search of him. He reached him just in time to take sad leave of him and lay him down in an easier posture. Turpin, murmuring contritely "*Mea culpa!*" raised his eyes and his folded hands towards heaven and, in a humble prayer for God's mercy, peacefully expired. Thus ended the warlike and pious Archbishop of Rheims, one of the boldest champions and most eloquent preachers of Christendom, who never ceased, while he had breath, to wage war against the heathens either with lance and sword or with most persuasive sermons.

Nothing ever had grieved Roland more, save only the death of his own Oliver. While his tears fell fast, he composed the prelate's body as decorously as he could on this rough death-bed; he crossed his hands, so fair and white, upon his breast,

ARCHBISHOP TURPIN, HIMSELF DYING, BLESSES THE DEAD PEERS LAID AT HIS FEET BY ROLAND. ROLAND BRINGS HIS FRIEND OLIVER'S BODY.

The Archbishop's Last Blessing

and sadly spoke a brief funeral oration:

"Go, thou knight of a noble race! I commit thee into the keeping of the Lord on high. For no man ever served Him more willingly. Not since the Apostles was seen such zeal to convert men and uphold Christendom. May thy soul be exempted from all pain and trials, and find the gate of Paradise wide open!"

VI

ROLAND'S DEATH

AND now behold Roland alone—the only living man upon that field of death! Would Charles arrive in time to exchange with him a last farewell? For, though unwounded, he knew that he must die, and that soon. Human endurance, of body or of mind, could no further go. He longed to lay him down and rest. But at least he would die on Spanish soil, on the land which, but for him, had never been subject to Charles. So he commended himself to the Archangel Gabriel, took his Olifant in one hand, and in the other Durendal, his sword, for from these two he would not be parted even in death, and slowly walking as far as the nearest Spanish field, ascended a low hill, or rather knoll, on which there grew some tall trees, and which rose leaning towards the high mountainside in four terraces, like steps cut in the rock. There, upon a green, grassy spot he sank down exhausted.

Now, among the bodies lying all around, there was a living Saracen, who only shammed death, the more surely to make his escape at nightfall. When he saw who it was that rested on that knoll, faint and nearly senseless, he rose up quickly and hurried to the spot, in the hope of earning at one stroke glory enough to last him his life. He laid violent hands on Roland, shouting: "Victory! he is down, Charles's terrible nephew, and I will have his sword to show at home!" With this he irreverently pulled Roland's beard and took hold of the sword's hilt.

But as he pulled, Roland suddenly awoke. Opening his eyes, he merely said, "I do not know thee for one of our men," and struck the bold miscreant such a blow upon the head with his Olifant as broke through the steel helmet and the skull, and stretched him dead at his feet.

"Cowardly fool!" said the hero, "what made thee so bold to lay hands on Roland! Now my Olifant is cleft, the gold and gems have all dropped out of it."

This incident aroused Roland to the danger that his sword, his precious Durendal, might, when he was dead, fall into the hands of some marauding Saracen, who not only would bear it away as a cheaply won trophy, but might even use it as a mute witness to a lying boast of having fought and slain its heroic owner. There was only one way to make such desecration absolutely impossible, and that was—to destroy the sword. In the full certainty that their joint labours were done forever, he set to work almost cheerfully to accomplish himself what, only the day before, would have been to him the greatest of heartaches short of the loss of a human friend. A little way from where he rested there was a low rock, of a hard, dark stone. On that he struck Durendal with all his might, blow after blow—in vain! The steel shrieked, but neither bent nor broke; the edge was not even

ROLAND TRYING TO BREAK DURENDAL AGAINST A ROCK; AND ROLAND BLOWING THE OLIFANT.

(From a Stained-Glass Window in the Cathedral at Chartres, France, XIIIth Century.)

dented. After a brief rest he tried again, and then again, for the third time; but each time the strokes were feebler, for his strength was ebbing fast. When he saw that he could not destroy his sword, his heart overflowed with pity, and he spoke to it sadly and tenderly:

"O my good Durendal, so bright and shining! how dost thou flash and sparkle in the sun! How well I mind the day when the great Emperor, with his own royal hand, did gird thee round my body! Since that day, how many countries have we two not won for him, thou and I together! How then should I not grieve at parting with thee now. Better die than leave thee to the Paynims. And certes, while I live, thou shalt not be taken from me. But after?—Oh, may God spare France this crowning disgrace! Let the holy relics, of which there are many in thy golden pommel, protect thee, my Durendal, so fair and holy, from their sacrilegious hands!"

Roland feels death creeping from his head to his heart. He lays himself down under a pine, with his Olifant and Durendal under him, so as to protect them with his body even after life has fled, and with his face turned towards Spain. In this mute fashion he would tell Charles that he died a conqueror still. He penitently strikes his breast, and makes his confession to God:

"*Mea culpa!* My God, by Thy great might and mercy, forgive my sins, little and great, all those I committed from the day of my birth, to this, the day of my death!"

God hears the noble knight, and sends His angels to soothe his anguish and ease his heart. His mind wanders and brings him memories of many things: his early home,—his own kinsfolk and friends,—the countries he has conquered,—and Charlemagne, his lord, who has nurtured him so tenderly, and loved him ever as a son. But he strives to recall his straying thoughts to his own urgent plight:

"O God, our true Father!" he prayed, "God, Who never didst lie, Who didst raise Lazarus from the dead, and protect Daniel

THE ARCHANGEL GABRIEL BLESSES THE DYING ROLAND.

(From a German MS., XIIth Century.)

against the lions,—save, Oh, save my soul and shield it against all perils, and forgive all the sins I ever committed!"

As he prays, he raises his hand to heaven, offering to God the glove from his right hand. Gabriel receives it; then he folds his hands, his head sinks gently on his shoulder. Angels and cherubs hover around him, and archangels—Raphael, and Michael, and Gabriel—bear his soul straight to Paradise.

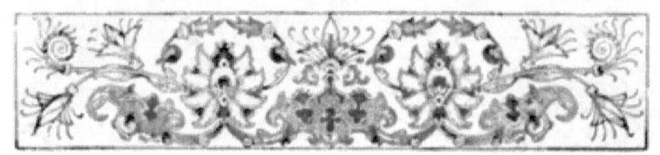

PART THIRD

RETRIBUTION

I

FIRST REPRISAL—CHARLEMAGNE'S DREAMS

ROLAND is dead, and God has his soul.

The Emperor, meanwhile, reached Roncevaux and rode into the pass. Not a road, or even path, not an empty space, not an ell or foot of ground, but there lay bodies of either French or Paynims.

"Where art thou," Charles exclaimed, "my well-beloved nephew? Where is the Archbishop? where are my twelve Peers, whom I have left behind?"

CHARLES VIEWS THE DEAD AT RONCEVAUX SEEKING FOR HIS NEPHEW ROLAND. (IN THE FOREGROUND, ARCHBISHOP TURPIN AND THE DEAD PEERS.)

But alas, what boots it to question where there are none to give reply?

There was great mourning that day in those gloomy defiles; wailing and weeping were heard everywhere, as men missed their sons, their brothers, their friends, or liege lords. Many dismounted and fell to the ground, overcome with grief. Old Duke Naimes was the first to rally from the shock, the first who ventured to speak to Charles.

"Look!" he said; "do you see that cloud of dust yonder, a few miles ahead of us? That is the Pagan host—there are still enough left of them. Ride on, fall on them from the rear, and avenge our dire disgrace."

The King partly roused himself at this, though he was half stunned with horror. He called to him four of his most trusty barons:

"Do you guard these valleys and these mountains. Leave the dead as they are; only watch that no beasts of prey come near them, knights and squires and serving men alike. I forbid you to let any man move or touch them until, by the grace of God, we return to you."

And he left a thousand knights with the four barons.

Then he ordered the trumpets sounded, and started in pursuit with all his army. But very soon the night began to fall, and riding, in those dark and narrow mountain gorges, became almost impossible. The Emperor dismounted, and kneeling on the grass, besought the Lord our God that He might stay the sun, keep back the night, and grant some more hours of light, When lo! the angel who was wont secretly to hold commune with the great monarch, stood by him invisible, and quickly whispered to him Heaven's command:

"Ride on, Charles! Daylight shall not fail thee. Thou hast this day lost the flower of French chivalry; God knows it, and bids thee go and take thy vengeance on the miscreant brood."

And God worked a great miracle for the King He loved: the sun stood arrested in its course, so the French could continue the pursuit and drive the Saracens before them towards Saragossa, making great slaughter of them, till they backed them against the river Ebro, where the current was deep and terribly swift. Not a boat, not a barge, not a ferry in sight! Yet there was nothing for them but to rush into the flood and try to swim across—a venture most desperate! The knights being most heavily armed, many of them sank at once and never came up. Of the others some floated and some drank deep before they reached the opposite bank; but the greater part were cruelly drowned.

When Charles saw that the victory was complete, he knelt again and gave thanks to God. When he arose, the sun had set. It was too late to return to Roncevaux; so the command was given to encamp, to free the tired horses from their harnesses, to take off their saddles and bits, and turn them loose to rest and graze in the luxuriant river-meadows. All slept wherever they dropped down, overcome with fatigue. Not even a watch was set that night.

The Emperor himself had a couch spread for him in a meadow, on the grass. But he would not disarm that night. He planted his lance in the ground by his head; he lay down in his shining mail-shirt and his golden, gem-studded helmet; he did not even loosen from his belt his sword Joyeuse,—that sword which never had its match, and gleamed, resplendent, with thirty different colours each day. In its golden pommel Charles had set the point of the holy lance with which the soldier pierced the side of Our Lord on the cross, and which, by a wondrous favour of Heaven, had come into his possession. Because of this high honour and of the steel's goodness, he called the sword, "Joyeuse," and from this name was formed his own royal battle-cry " Mountjoy!" which French barons have shouted on many a field long after he was dead.

Through all this still, moonlit night Charles, though mortally tired with the exertions and emotions of that fateful day, could find no sleep. If he closed his eyes, he saw before him that dreadful pass heaped full with the bodies of his friends; he called on Oliver, on his Peers, and there, tossing upon his unrestful couch, he prayed with tears and sobs that God might have mercy on all those faithful souls. No one kept the sorrowful vigil with the King; wherever he looked he saw sleeping men; the very horses were too weary to stand; if any wanted the tempting grass, they just stretched their necks and nibbled as they lay. At last, towards dawn, Charles fell into the sleep of utter exhaustion, and the Archangel Gabriel, sent by God, kept watch over him and brought him warnings and advice in dreams, as so many times before.

The Angel first showed him the vision of a great battle, then pointed heavenward. Glancing up, Charles beheld among the clouds lightnings, thunderbolts, hail and showers, terrific storms and conflagrations, and the next instant it seemed as though it all came down upon his army. The shields and lance-shafts caught fire, the hauberks and helmets began to melt and drop off the men. And now a band of bears and leopards rushes upon them, and with them serpents, dragons, flying and crawling monsters, and thousands of griffins. .All cry to the King for help; he fain would fly to the rescue, but an immense lion springs out of a forest and stands right across his path, fierce and aggressive. The beast attacks the King— they wrestle—which will prevail? Charles never knew, for the vision somehow vanished. Yet the King did not awake.

And now another vision. He is at home, in his city of Aix. He stands on the porch of his palace, holding a bear by a double chain. Suddenly thirty bears come out of the forest. They speak like men. "Give him back to us!" they entreat. "He is of our kin and we are bound to help him. It is not right to keep him captive so long." But just then a fine deer-hound comes running and bounding from the palace and attacks the largest of the bears. And Charles, with bated breath looks on at the stupendous combat. Which will be victor? Again he does not know, for this vision, too, vanishes like the first.

These things did the Angel show the King. And now he slept till morning.

II

SCENES AT SARAGOSSA

KING MARSILIUS, meanwhile, flying for his life, reached Saragossa. There, dismounting under an olive tree, he let his servitors disarm him—take from him his sword, his helmet, and hauberk; then, silently and most piteously, stretched himself on the grass. The pain and loss of blood from his severed wrist were so great, there having been neither time nor means to dress the wound properly, that he fainted away. His Queen, Bramimonda and her women surrounded him with tears and cries, but neither they nor any of the twenty thousand men with him seemed able to collect their wits sufficiently to lend him efficient aid. All they could do was to wail and moan, to curse

Charles and France, and lastly to abuse their god Apollo, whose statue was in a grotto near by. Thither they rushed, tore from the statue sceptre and crown, threw it down on the ground, kicked and trampled it under foot, beat it with sticks and broke it to pieces, scolding and reviling it the while: "Thou wicked god! Why didst thou shame us so? Why didst thou leave our King to suffer? Is it even so thou dost requite them that have always served thee well?" The effigy of Mahomet was cast into a ditch for dogs and hogs to trample and worry. Never were gods treated with such indignity. When Marsilius awoke from his swoon, he had himself carried to his own chamber, whither Queen Bramimonda followed him, still weeping and tearing her hair, and calling down all manner of evils on Charles and the French.

"Our only hope now," she said, "is the Emir."

This Emir was Baligant, the Sovereign of Babylon, an old man of high repute in heathendom. Marsilius had, some time before, sent to him for help, threatening, if he failed him, to forswear his pagan gods, to receive the Christian law, and make his peace with Charlemagne. But Babylon is far, and the Emir had not been heard from yet. He had, however, gone to work at once collecting ships and men, and on the first of May his fleet had set sail from the port of Alexandria in Egypt. It was a beautiful sight, especially of a dark night, when the sea was illumined with the lights burning at every mast-head, at the end of every yard-arm. It was thus the fleet arrived in sight of the Spanish coast; the radiancy stretched over miles of shore and carried the happy news to the discouraged towns and villages, from whence it swiftly spread inland and soon reached Marsilius,—yet hardly sooner than the fleet itself, which entered into the mouths of the river Ebro, and made with all speed for Saragossa, amazing the country with the prodigious brilliancy of its thousands of lights, which, along both banks of the river, turned the night into day.

A short distance from Saragossa the Emir ordered the fleet to halt and went on shore, accompanied by all the chiefs of the army and a gorgeous retinue of noble warriors. In the middle of a plain, under a laurel tree, a large rug was spread, an ivory armchair was placed on that, and Baligant took his seat, while all the others remained standing. He began to speak in the most overbearing way of how he would make short work of Charles and all Christendom, how he would follow him even to the city of Aix—"and," he concluded, "if he does not prostrate himself at my feet and sue for mercy, and deny the Christian faith, I shall tear the crown from his head. I vow I shall not cease from this emprise until I see him either dead, or a suppliant."

With this comforting message he dispatched two of his nobles to King Marsilius. They quickly covered the short distance to the city, and after passing ten gates and four bridges, rode along the streets, through gaping crowds, straight for the royal palace on the hill. The nearer they came to that, the louder grew the uproar, and they gradually began to make out the plaints and threats in which the angry multitude gave vent to their excited feelings.

The messengers left their horses in the shade of an olive tree, where two Saracens took charge of them, and were shown to the royal chamber at the top of the palace. As they entered the King's presence, they uttered the customary greeting: "May Apollo and Mahomet, our lord, save the King and guard the Queen!" and were greatly amazed when, instead of the usual courteous response, and, indeed, against every law of Oriental etiquette, the Queen, without giving her lord a chance to speak, broke out into the most furious invectives:

"What nonsense are you talking? Do you not know that those worthless gods of ours are dastardly felons, who left all our knights to perish at Roncevaux, and did not even protect the King, my lord! Roland, the mighty champion, met him in battle and cut off his right hand. Ah, miserable me! unhappy woman that I am! what will become of me, when Charles is in possession of all Spain? Is there no one who in pity will take my life?"

"Lady," said the messengers, "moderate your words. We are the envoys of the Emir Baligant, who has come with an immense army to be your deliverer: see the token—glove and wand—which he sends Marsilius. Down there on the river we have four thousand vessels—transports, light skiffs and swift galleys. The Emir is wealthy and powerful. He will—so he swears—pursue Charles and attack him in his own land, and never rest till he sees him either dead or a suppliant."

"Do not deceive yourselves," she replied, despondently; "things will not go so smoothly. You will not have to go so far to encounter the French. These seven years they have been here, right in our land. And as for their Emperor—all the kings of the earth are to him as infants, and he fears no living man."

"Enough!" here broke in Marsilius, bethinking himself at last that he was playing no dignified part, and addressing the envoys: "Lords, it is to me you must speak. You see yourselves in what mortal straits I am. I have no son, no heir. Yesterday I had one—they killed him. Tell the Emir to come to me, for I cannot go to him. He has the next claim to the land of Spain. If he so wishes, I will give it up to him at once,—only let him defend it against the French. I shall be able to give him some useful hints, which may help him to victory. In the meantime take to him the keys of Saragossa and tell him from me he need not leave this neighbourhood."

"You speak well," said the envoys, and, after receiving the keys, and respectfully saluting the King, they took horse at once and, riding hard, in great trepidation, returned to the Emir, to whom they faithfully recounted all they had seen and the portentous things they had heard. He listened in silence, and for some time sat as one stunned, till they reminded him that, if the losses of their allies had been great, neither had the French come off cheaply.

"Remember," they said, "Roland was killed, and so was Oliver. Dead are the twelve Peers whom Charles loved so dearly, and twenty thousand French besides. Now, Charles and his army are encamped here by the river, close to us, and you can make retreat very hard for them."

The old Paynim's eyes gleamed fiercely at these words; he sprang from his chair, and gave his orders, quick and brief:

"Lose not an instant more! Land all the troops; then—to horse, and forward! on! Unless old Charlemagne escapes us by flight, Marsilius shall be avenged this very day. For the hand he has lost, I will give him the Emperor's head."

The Emir superintended both the landing and the mustering of the troops, and as soon as he had seen them ready to start and committed the command of them to his most trusty captain, he rode, with only four companions, to the city and the palace. At the top of the stairs he was met by Bramimonda, who rushed out of the royal chamber and fell at his feet in most pitiable plight. He raised her kindly, and both together entered the chamber.

Marsilius, as soon as he saw the Emir enter, called two Saracens to him, to raise him in their arms. Then, taking one of his gloves in his left hand, he held it out to the noble visitor, saying:

"My lord Emir, I here deliver into your hand my entire kingdom. As for me, I am a wreck, and I have lost my people."

"Believe me," replied the Emir, "I sorrow for you deeply. But I may not tarry to talk, for Charles will not wait for me."

With a brief farewell, and tears in his eyes at so much misery, Baligant left the room, quickly descended the marble stairs, mounted his horse, and was soon in the front of his army, whom he cheered on with the frequent exclamation:

"On! on! Let not the French escape!"

III

THE OBSEQUIES

WHEN Charles the Emperor awoke that morning, soon after daybreak, the Archangel Gabriel, whom God had deputed to watch over him in his slumber, raised his hand and made over him the sacred sign in blessing, ere he returned to the spheres of eternal light. With the Emperor arose his knights, refreshed and rested, and all rode back to Roncevaux, to examine the doleful place of the great massacre. When Charles came upon the first dead, his tears began to flow, and turning to them that rode nearest to him he said:

"Dear knights, walk your horses awhile. I must ride on alone, for I would fain find my nephew Roland myself. One day at Aix, at an annual festival, I remember my valiant bachelors were boasting of their feats, the hard fights in which they had been, and Roland (I heard him) said that if it ever were his fate to die in a foreign country, his body should be found in advance of his peers and of his men, with the face turned towards the enemy's land, for even in death he still would be a conqueror."

So saying, Charles rode on, a stone's throw ahead of his companions, up a hill.

And as he rode slowly, looking every way, he noticed that the hillside was covered with herbs and flowers, all dyed in his barons' red heart-blood. Deeply moved at the sight, he halted on the top of the hill, under the two trees. He first discovered the rock, on which he knew the trace left by the blows which Roland had struck with Durendal, and there, close by, he came upon Roland himself, stretched out on the green grass. The next minute he was off his horse, and taking the beloved body in his arms, held it to his breast an instant, then fell with it in a dead swoon,

When he returned to consciousness, Duke Naimes and three other barons had raised, and were supporting him. He gazed down upon the countenance so dear to him, marvelling much, for though Roland's cheek and brow and lips had lost their ruddy colour, he still had a look so fair and serene, almost as of life; and the King began to speak to him so feelingly that all who heard him wept with excess of grief:

"Friend Roland, may God receive thy soul and rest it amid holy flowers of Paradise with the host of his glorious elect! Why, oh, why was it decreed that thou shouldst come to Spain? Never, as long as I live, shall a day pass on which I mourn not for thee. What care I now for power, for glory, when all my joy has passed from me! Who will be my support and stay? What friends have I under heaven? None! My sons? There is not one that can compare with him. Friend Roland, I now must return to France. When I shall be in my city of Aix, strangers will come from many lands, and ask for thee. And I shall answer, 'He died in Spain.' And lo! they will all rebel against me—Saxons, Hungarians, Bulgars, and numberless other peoples. And I shall miss thee more each day. Ah, truly, France, sweet France! art thou orphaned this day. As for me, so great is my sorrow, I would that I could die—die here and now, in these most fatal passes, that my soul might join all these loyal souls and my body be buried with theirs."

The aged King was very near swooning again; his trembling hands unconsciously tore at his hair and beard as, with broken voice, he spoke a last blessing and farewell.

"Friend Roland, and art thou gone indeed? Ah me, thy young life is done. May thy soul find joy in Paradise!"

The barons looked at one another in dismay. They feared lest excessive grief might unman their aged liege, and felt that something must be done to rouse him to action of some sort. Geoffrey of Anjou was the first to speak—one of the

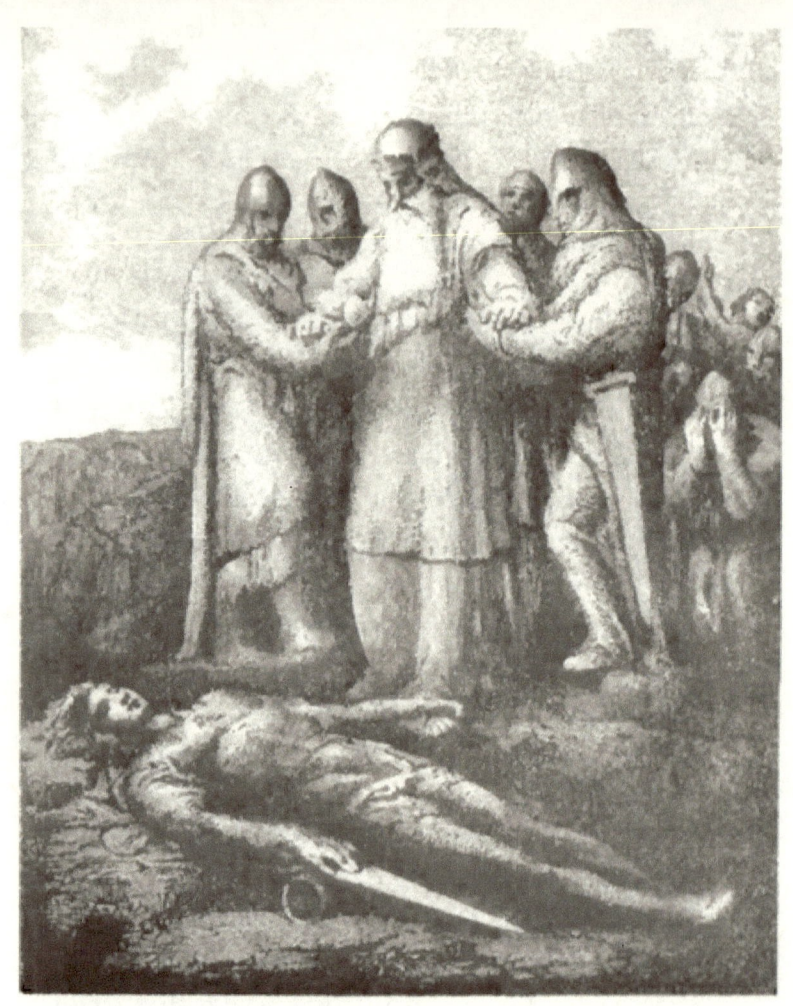

CHARLES MOURNS OVER ROLAND'S BODY.

four who were supporting him in this hour of weakness.

"Sir King," he said, "yield not your soul entirely to grief; much there is that should be looked to. Will you not command that out of all these dead our own be sought out and laid in a common tomb?"

"You are right," replied Charles, partly rousing himself. "Sound your horn!"

All was done as Geoffrey suggested. In the army there was no lack of bishops, abbots, priests, and monks, to give the dead absolution and benison. Then great quantities were burned of incense and of myrrh; the bodies were interred with every honour and left forever in those mountain wilds—for what else could the sorrowing friends have done?

By the Emperor's order, the bodies of Roland, Oliver, and Turpin were laid apart. After the general obsequies, he had them opened in his presence. The hearts were wrapped each in a silk cloth and placed in white marble caskets. The bodies were carefully washed with wine and spices, and sewed up in deer hides, then each was laid on a chariot and covered with a pall of precious Oriental silk, and the three chariots followed the army, under strong and honourable escort.

Just as all these sad rites had been attended to, and Charles was preparing to depart, there suddenly appeared, at a turn of the winding pass, the vanguard of the Saracens. Two heralds rode out from the front rank, and thus, in the Emir's name, challenged the King to battle:

"Thou proud King! no way of escape is open to thee. Baligant is here, having ridden in thy track. Countless the host he brings from Araby. This day will show what stuff ye are made of, thou and thy men."

Nothing could have happened more opportunely to rouse Charles from his despondent mood. He cast a glance of pride over his army, and, without deigning to give the Paynim messengers a direct reply, shouted in loud, defiant tones:

"To horse, ye barons! to arms and to horse!"

IV

ROLAND AVENGED

THE Emperor was the first to arm himself, and when, mounted on his best charger, he galloped along his army's front, calling aloud on God and St. Peter, he was cheered with wild enthusiasm, and there was but one cry through the ranks:

"This man was born to wear a crown!"

He called to him Duke Naimes and Count Josseran of Provence; these two experienced captains he appointed to muster and divide the army in columns, which they did most promptly and skilfully. The vanguard they left as it was,—two columns, composed entirely of French knights. In the third column they placed the brave Bavarians, thirty thousand in all, under Ogier, the renowned

Paladin of Denmark. Then came the knights from other parts of Germany, all with strong horses and excellent arms and most stubborn spirit. The fifth column was composed of Normans under their own Duke Richard, and the sixth of men from Brittany. Then came those from Auvergne and Poitou in one body—the seventh—and the barons from Flanders in the eighth, while the ninth was formed of knights from Burgundy and Lorraine.

The tenth column was the choicest; it was composed of the oldest barons of France, with snowy locks and beards, in resplendent armours; their shields all covered with various cognizances. With them rode Charlemagne himself, and Geoffrey of Anjou, who bore the royal standard, the noble Oriflamme.

When the army stood ordered thus in perfect battle array, Charles dismounted, and kneeling on the grass, his face turned to the rising sun, he poured out his heart in a fervent prayer:

"O Thou, Who art our true Father, be thou my shield this day! Thou Who

AN OLIFANT (XIITH CENTURY).

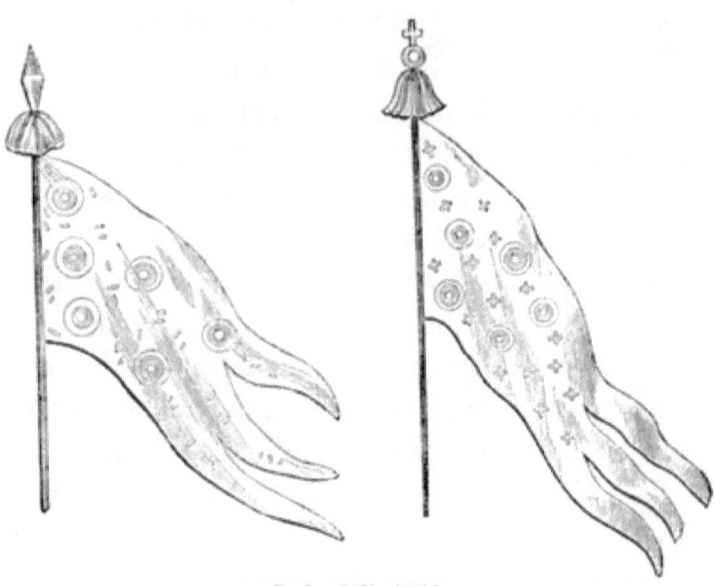

THE ORIFLAMME.
(*After Mosaics in the Basilica of St. John Lateran in Rome, IXth Century.*)

Roland Avenged

didst save Jonah from the monster's maw and spare the King of Nineveh with his city and all his people,—Thou Who didst deliver Daniel from the ravenous lions, and didst preserve the three youths in the blazing furnace,—let Thy loving care encompass me to-day, and of Thy goodness grant, if such thy pleasure, that I may avenge my nephew Roland!"

Having ended his prayer, Charles rose from his knees, making on his brow the sign of the all-conquering Cross, then mounted, while Duke Naimes and Josseran held his stirrup. He never had looked more handsome, noble, cheery, more altogether royal, never had managed his steed with more chivalrous grace. He spread his white beard broadly over his chest, and so did his guard of honour, for love of him.

At that instant the clarions were sounded at front and rear; Roland's Olifant rang out loudest and clearest above the rest. The sound brought tears again to many an eye and fired each heart with double eagerness for the coming battle, which all felt would be decisive. It was therefore in the most promising mood that they hurried on through that wilderness of precipitous mountains, of beetling rocks and narrow valleys, out into open ground on the Spanish side of the pass. There, in the middle of an immense plain, they halted waiting for the attack. And the Emir's scouts hastened to their master with the tidings:

"We have seen Charles, that proud King; fierce are his men, and not one will fail him at the proof. Quick, arm yourself! Make ready!"

The Paynim army thrice exceeded the Christian host in numbers. It was divided into thirty columns which included all the nations of the East and all those in Europe which had not been conquered by Charlemagne. Of the former, there were troops from Egypt, Nubia, Arabia, Persia, Palestine; among the latter there were Hungarians, Serbs and other Slavs, Prussians, and many other heathen barbarians. So that it is hardly to be wondered at if the Emir, riding from rank to rank on his fiery Arabian courser, in all the splendour of Oriental armament, felt and inspired the most absolute confidence in his power to crush the Christians at one blow. He even yet did not quite believe that they would actually accept his challenge.

"Charles," he said to his son who was riding close behind him with other captains, "Charles is mad to dare this venture. If he does not refuse the battle, he will never again wear golden crown on his brow."

But the Christians stood in battle array, and there could be no doubt that they meant to fight. And never was field more apt. Vast and perfectly level, it was not broken by a single wood or mound; nothing that could serve as cover or for an ambush, or conceal the movements of one army from the other, even for a moment. Had Roland had such a field, things would have gone very differently. The day, too, was fair and unclouded, and when the Emir led the charge with his three standard-bearers, there was nothing in either place or weather that favoured one army more than the other. Both were in the highest spirits and so fiercely resolute, nothing but death could have separated them.

Charles himself was in the thickest of the fray, alert and active as any younger knight; but for him Duke Naimes would not have seen the night, having been unhorsed and stunned by a terrible blow struck on his head by a noted Saracen warrior, the Emir's brother, just as he had slain in single combat the Emir's own son. Charles chanced to be in that part of the field. He rode down the Saracen champion so furiously, striking him with his lance full in the breast, that he dropped from his horse without a word. The King then raised his old friend, gently helped him into the saddle, and led him to a quieter spot. The old warrior took but a short rest and soon was in the hottest of it again, with Ogier of Denmark, whose prowess that day outdid even his own former achievements, and Geoffrey of Anjou, the noble bearer of the Oriflamme. On the whole, in spite of great losses, the day went well for the Christians, and Roland's Olifant, sounding high above all other horns and clarions, seemed to taunt the Paynims with its exulting notes.

Baligant, maddened with rage at the death of his son and his brother, was riding all over the field in search of Charles. Nothing would satisfy him but a personal engagement with the King himself. It was only towards dusk that he at last had his wish. They met in the very middle of the field, shouting each his battle-cry. The encounter was not unequal, for both were of about the same age, and most evenly matched for valour and warlike skill. Their feelings, too, were equally high-wrought, one being passionately desirous of avenging his nephew, the other his son. At the first shock, both shields were shattered just above the buckle, and the mail-shirts were ripped as though they had been of silk. At the same instant the girths of both chargers snapped apart, the saddles turned, and both champions found themselves on the ground, but promptly sprang to their feet and drew their swords.

"Thou didst kill my son," said Baligant as he sought for a break in the armour, where his sword's point might enter; "and most unjustly didst invade my land. Still, if thou wilt do homage to me, I will give it thee in fief."

"It were deadly shame," replied Charles, as he parried stroke after stroke. "I owe a heathen neither love nor troth; yet will I love thee, if thou but accept God's law and become a Christian."

"Idle words!" cried the Emir; "swords are better."

And with that he aimed a cut at Charles's head with such violence and precision that the sword went through the helmet of burnished steel, and slashed off the hair on one side and a slice of the flesh the breadth of a hand, so that the bone was laid bare. The King swayed on his feet and might have fallen again, but suddenly Gabriel, the Archangel, stood at his side, invisible to all but him; and he heard his warning voice:

"Great King, bethink thee! Lose not thyself!"

The instant that Charles saw the heavenly form and heard the inspiring words, all fear of death left him, his strength revived tenfold; with his own peerless sword he struck his foe's helmet all sparkling with gems, and while the Emir staggered, stunned under the blow, cleft his skull down to the white beard and left him dead on the field. Then, shouting "Mountjoy!" he raised his great stature for his men to know him. Duke Naimes rushed for his charger, and held him for the King to mount, no one hindering, for the Paynims, seeing the Emir fall, had fled, panic-stricken, and scattered all over the plain.

Charles at once ordered the pursuit.

"Chase them!" he shouted to his barons; "God gives them into your hands. Take your fill of vengeance, relieve your hearts! Pay them for the tears which I have seen you shed this morning!"

The chase was hot, and great the slaughter; very few escaped.

The heat had been oppressive. Yet the townsmen had watched the changing fortunes of the day from the city walls, as much as they could see through the whirling clouds of dust. All day Queen Bramimonda had hardly left her tower, where she stood with her women and many priests of her false faith. When she saw the rout of the Paynim army, and the Christians riding hard after them, even under the city walls, she rushed into Marsilius' chamber, forgetful of his pitiful condition, crying in dire despair:

"O noble King! our men are beaten! The Emir is dead—perished ignominiously!"

At the cruel tidings thus ruthlessly conveyed, the poor weak King turned to the wall and, covering his face with his hands to hide the streaming tears, expired without a word.

That same night the victors slept in Saragossa, peacefully and unafraid, well knowing that no further defence would be attempted. The Queen herself delivered the keys into Charles's own hands.

The next day, by the Emperor's order, a thousand knights patrolled the streets in all directions, entering every mosque they came across, and breaking up with mallets and maces all the unholy images. When this work of pious destruction was thoroughly done, the bishops consecrated the waters of the river and the fountains, and set about baptising the inhabitants, and if one refused to do Charles's bidding and was obdurate, he was either hanged, cut down, or burned. In this way over one hundred thousand were baptised and became good Christians. Only Queen Bramimonda was let alone for the present, because Charles intended to take her home with him to France, and there to have her instructed and converted gently, by loving persuasion.

One thousand valiant knights were left as garrison; then the Emperor, with the entire army, started homeward. They halted for a day at Bordeaux, the great city at the mouth of the Gironde. There, in the cathedral church, Charles laid Roland's Olifant, well filled with gold coin, upon the main altar, and for many years pilgrims could see it there. He crossed the wide Gironde in ships, and stopped on his way only once more, at the abbey where the obsequies of the three noble champions, Roland, Oliver, and the Archbishop, were celebrated with the Church's most solemn pomp, their bodies laid to rest in white marble tombs, and their souls commended once more, with a last farewell, to God and all His saints. After this Charles never halted until he dismounted at the wide porch of his own palace at Aix. He hardly took the time to rest before he dispatched messengers to summon wise men from all the countries subject to him—Saxony and Bavaria, Burgundy and Lorraine and Germany, Brittany and Normandy, and others—to form a royal court of justice, together with the wisest among the French barons, for the trial of the traitor Ganelon.

V

THE TRAITOR'S PUNISHMENT

AS the Emperor, arriving at his city of Aix, ascended the stairs of his palace, he was met in the great hall by a damsel tall and fair. It was Aude, Oliver's sister and Roland's affianced wife.

"Where is Roland the Captain?" she demanded of Charles. "Where is he who swore to take me for his bride?"

Charles was dumb with sorrow and sympathy for the maiden, and his fingers pulled at his beard, as was his wont whenever he was much moved.

"Sister, dear friend!" he answered at last, "thou askest for one who is dead. But do not pine, for I will make good thy loss. I will give thee Louis, my own son, and heir to all my lands. What more can I say?"

"Such words, in sooth, sound strangely to my ear," fair Aude replied. "God, and His saints, and His angels forefend that, Roland dead, I should live!"

Even as she spoke, the colour faded from her cheek, and she sank down at the feet of the King. He thought she had swooned and, bending over her with pitying, tearful eyes and endearing words, took her hands and tried to raise her. But her head fell limply on her shoulder; all plainly saw that life had fled. The barons stood awestruck, and not many eyes were dry as they devoutly murmured a prayer for the gentle soul. The King ordered four ladies of the court to bear her to a nunnery, where they watched by her all night and until daybreak, when she was interred by the altar in the church, with great honours.

And now there was nothing in the way to delay the great trial. Ganelon the traitor was brought before the palace, loaded with iron chains. There he was bound to a strong post, his hands being tied with thongs of raw deer-hide. And

DEMOISELLE AUDE KILLED BY THE TIDINGS OF ROLAND'S DEATH.

all who would, beat him with sticks and whips. In such miserable plight did he await his trial. But his wicked spirit was even yet unbroken.

It was a great day and a general festival, when the great court assembled and the Emperor commanded the traitor to be brought before him. Charles opened the court in a brief and pithy address:

"My lords and barons! I pray you that you try Ganelon as is right and lawful. He went with me to Spain. He caused the death of twenty thousand French knights. He caused the death of Roland, my nephew, whom ye shall never see again. He caused the death of Oliver, the valiant and the courteous. In a word, he has, for money, betrayed my twelve Peers."

"All this is true," said Ganelon, undaunted and defiant, "and may I be accursed if I deny it. But Roland had wronged me of much gold and silver. Hence it was I wished for his death and worked his ruin. But I do not admit my action to have been treason."

Ganelon, as he spoke these monstrous words, stood proud and straight before the King. His cheek was ruddy, and his bearing confident. With a quick, sharp glance he took in the hall and the court of his peers, and the crowd of those who came to see and hear. Among these last he detected thirty of his own kinsmen. This marvellously enhanced his courage, and he now spoke out quite boldly:

"For the love of God, barons, hear me! True, I was in the Emperor's army, and I served him loyally and lovingly. But his nephew Roland had a grudge against me, and as good as condemned me to death. He got the King to send me as messenger to Marsilius, and if I escaped, it was through my own cleverness. Then I challenged Roland and Oliver and all their companions. Charles and his noble barons were witnesses to the challenge. I call this vengeance, not treason."

"We will consult on this," said the judges.

Among Ganelon's thirty kinsmen there was one named Pinabel, a notable warrior and a no less notable speaker, never at a loss for an argument. To him said Ganelon:

"It is to you I look to deliver me from disgrace and death."

"I will be your champion," Pinabel readily replied. "The first man who votes for your death—I challenge him to mortal combat. The Emperor must give us time and place, and my sword shall prove the man a liar."

In the meantime, the court had retired to consider the verdict. Those of the barons who were more leniently inclined and better disposed towards Pinabel gradually won a hearing:

"Better let the matter rest. Let us stop the trial and pray the King this once to pardon Ganelon, who will henceforth serve him faithfully and without guile. Roland is dead; you cannot call him back. Nor can gold or silver bring him back. As to this combat, 't were folly to permit it."

All the barons assented, save only Thierri, the brother of Geoffrey of Anjou.

The barons now returned into Charlemagne's presence:

"Sire," they said, "we pray you, hold Count Ganelon acquitted. He will henceforth serve you faithfully and lovingly. Let him live; for he is of very noble lineage. Roland, moreover, is dead; we shall never see him more. Nor will gold or silver bring him back."

"Ye are traitors, all of you!" cried the King, angrily, and seeing that all were against him, he bowed his head, exclaiming, "Oh, miserable me!"

Suddenly a knight stood before him— Thierri, Duke Geoffrey's brother, of middle stature, sparely built and dark, with black hair and brown eyes. Courteously he addressed Charles:

"Be not so grieved, Sir King! You know I have always served you well, and now my ancestry entitles me to sit in this court. In whatever way Roland may have wronged Ganelon, your interest should have been his protection. Ganelon sold him—he is a felon. He has perjured himself right here before you. For all this I condemn him to a traitor's death: let him be hanged and his body thrown to the dogs. If he have a kinsman who be willing to give me the lie, with this my sword I am ready to maintain my say."

"He speaks well," said the French.

Then Pinabel came forth and stood before the King: tall, broad, and of such strength that he could kill a man with one blow of his fist.

"Sire," he said, "this is your court; you preside. Forbid them then to make so much noise. The thing is simple: Thierri has pronounced his sentence; I give him the lie and challenge him to mortal combat. Here my token!"

And he presents to Charles his right-hand glove.

"So be it," said the Emperor; "but I must have good hostages besides."

Thirty of Pinabel's kinsmen immediately offered themselves.

"I too will give you pledges," said the King, and placed the hostages under strong guard, to await the result of the combat,

Thierri also gave his glove to Charles, who furnished hostages for him also, and commissioned Ogier of Denmark to order all the details.

The two champions heard mass, confessed their sins, and received holy communion after being absolved and blessed by a priest, and leaving ample alms to various churches; then armed themselves most carefully, and reported themselves ready to await the King's pleasure.

The combat took place in a vast plain just outside of Aix, where there was room for the immense crowd which streamed out to witness it. At the very first shock both champions were unhorsed, and for some time, in the fury of the mutual onslaught, it was impossible to predict the issue. Neither seemed to gain any advantage, and the anxiety of Charles and the French barons increased with every moment, till Charles exclaimed in deep anguish of mind, "O God! show us where is the right!"

"Surrender, Thierri!" Pinabel whispered to his adversary at a moment when they had been brought by the chances of the combat to very close quarters. "I am willing to become thy vassal, and serve thee loyally as my liege, and I will give thee of my wealth as much as thy heart desires—only make Ganelon's peace with the King!"

"Far be the thought from me!" replied Thierri. "Shame on me, were I to consent! No! Let God decide between us this day! Rather do thou give up the fight. Thou art strong and skilled in war; thy peers know thee well for a valiant man. I will make thy peace with Charles. But Ganelon must be brought to justice."

"God the Lord forbid!" cried Pinabel. "I intend to uphold my kindred, and yield to no mortal man. Better die than take such shame upon myself!"

After this parley the fight was resumed with greater violence still, and did not last much longer. At one moment Thierri, wounded in the face and nearly disarmed, all but his sword, was in imminent peril; but the next, rushing at Pinabel with the greater fury, he shattered his helmet and skull with one desperate stroke and felled him to the ground, dead.

Then a great shout went up to heaven :

"A miracle! a great miracle! God has shown the right! Now it is but just that Ganelon be hanged, he and all his kinsmen who have gone security for him!"

Charles, with four of his most illustrious barons—old Duke Naimes, Ogier of Denmark, Duke Geoffrey of Anjou, and William of Blaye—hastens to the spot where the victor stands, still dazed and sore hurt. He clasps Thierri in his arms, wipes the blood from his face with his own sable mantle. With great gentleness the champion is disarmed and placed upon a soft-paced mule of Araby, and joyously escorted back to Aix, there to be tenderly cared for.

Then Charles called together once more his counts and barons :

"What do you advise about the hostages who have been kept in durance?"

"Death! let them all die!" was the unanimous cry.

The cruel sentence was instantly executed. Thus a traitor not only ruins himself, but involves others in his ruin.

As for Ganelon himself, the hatred of the French was so intense, nothing would satisfy them but that he should die a horrible death of unheard-of torture: he was torn limb from limb by four wild horses, to the tails of which he had been strongly bound.

When this dreadful act of vengeance had been executed, Charles summoned learned bishops from France, Bavaria, and Germany, who were staying at his Court, and said to them:

"There is in my household a captive lady of high lineage. Since she is with us she has heard so many pious sermons and seen so many examples of holiness, that she wishes to believe in God and be a good Christian. Therefore, and that her soul may be saved, baptise her, I pray."

"Right willingly," they replied; "select her godmothers from among the noblest dames."

Thus it came to pass that, in presence of an immense crowd, Marsilius' widowed queen was baptised by the name of Juliana. She was a sincere and willing convert.

That night Charles, wearied with the day's manifold emotions and events, laid himself down in his high-vaulted chamber to rest and sleep. After these many years of toil and danger, he longed to spend some time at peace in his own beloved city, and work quietly with his learned clerks and schoolmen for the good and instruction of his people. But it was not to be. Rest was not for him who could do needful work in the world which no other man was equal to. In the dead of night God's messenger, the Archangel Gabriel, stood by his bedside once more, and bade him hasten without delay to some distant Eastern lands, to rescue Christians from oppressing infidels. The aged monarch groaned. "O God! how toilsome is my life!" he exclaimed, and wished that he might stay. But he never thought of disobeying the divine command. And forthwith, the next day, he began to prepare for another campaign, another war.

NOTE ON THE "CHANSON DE ROLAND"

DOES a curious student of times and manners wish he could conjure from the past a live piece out of the Middle Ages, with its rude feudal chivalry? let him pass by the shelffuls of "histories," and take up the "Chanson de Roland." There they all rise before him—acting, feeling, living flesh and blood—the typical *dramatis personæ* who make up the cast of the great play that fills the European stage during the millennium which it took the decadent ancient world to evolve into the modern world: the ideal King, wise and brave and pious; the Hero, the Friend, the noble Churchman, both learned and warlike, equally good at converting men by eloquent preaching or the no less persuasive sword; the Traitor, the Average Man of the time; and, lastly, the Foe, the Paynim, embodying the everlasting antagonism between the East and West. What matters it that every page bristles with historical incongruities, that facts and dates are jumbled into inextricable confusion? Those are little matters which can be set straight in a minute by looking into the briefest text-book, the most condensed cyclopædia, or dictionary of dates. But the colour, the vigour, the reality, the telling touch, the life, in a word—what book of references, what well-written history even, will give those?

And yet, the very truth of the poem makes it, if not exactly repulsive, still slightly disappointing, because it dispels much of the glamour, the fictitious romance, which a certain too indiscriminately enthusiastic poetical school has cast over mediæval life. No, they are not romantic, those fierce men-at-arms, for whom killing and being killed is the most natural occupation, "all in the day's work," and who give a thought to their wives and daughters incidentally, between two campaigns.

He is not romantic, Roland, the hero himself, who quarrels with his wiser friend out of sheer boastful recklessness, the foolish "punctilio" which the French have dubbed by the untranslatable name, *point d'honneur*, thereby sacrificing thousands of lives committed to his care; above all, he is not romantic, in the attractive sense of the word, in his relation to fair Aude, his affianced bride, no thought of whom crosses his mind even in the clear vision of the hour before death. He falls to "thinking of many things": the castle where his early youth was spent; his wars and conquests; the royal uncle who loved him—many dying visions, but not that of the fair girl who falls dead on hearing the news of his death! And these men, crimson to their necks with gore, on horses wading up to their bellies in warm blood—they are not romantic, still less poetical. But then we must remember that the "Lay of Roland" is preëminently a "military epic," as it has been aptly classed, presenting only one aspect of mediæval life, and, furthermore, that there is romance and poetry enough, of an elevating, manly sort, in the feelings which underlie and prompt the action : the simple but vigorous faith ; the self-forgetful devotion to the "liege lord," who embodies the idea of "country, native land," and, by his personal qualities, attaches men to himself by the noblest of bonds ; the loyalty of man to man, the tendernesss in friendship.

It must be admitted that this—to us the least attractive—"military" side of a great epoch must have appealed most strongly to the general sympathies, judging from the great and enduring popularity of the Roland epic through all the countries which were overshadowed by Charlemagne's gigantic personality, and from the countless transformations which the original subject-matter experienced in successive centuries at the hands of every description of second-hand versifiers.

There are few literary phenomena which arouse more curiosity than the evolution of a national epic. But of all such epics the "Roland" is perhaps the only one which affords a chance of tracing this evolution step by step.

Léon Gautier, the most exhaustive student, critic, editor, and translator (into modern French) of the *Chanson*, thus sums up in a masterly introduction the conditions which must combine to form a soil fit for a national epic to grow on :

> "If lyrical poetry is essentially personal, epic poetry is essentially national. It can grow only out of a people which is already a nation, with a national consciousness, and which combines four qualities not rare to find in simple times : it must be religiously inclined, warlike, unsophisticated (*naïve*), and fond of song. I may add that the nation should not, at the moment it produces the epic, be in a calm and prosperous condition : peace never yet gave birth to an epic. It needs a struggle, its birthplace is a battle-field, amidst the dying who have given their lives to some great cause. So much for soil. Then the epic needs matter—some positive, central fact, which it will enlarge upon in telling it. The fact is almost always historical, and mostly sad—a defeat, a death. . . . Lastly, it must have a hero, and the hero must completely embody his time and nationality. His personality must tower above the epic fact, so that this fact be nothing without him and derive all its importance from him."

This is all of reality that is needed. All the rest—and that is not little—is left to imagination, — elaboration of detail, of characters, amplification, and invention of incidents, etc.

All these conditions exist with marvellous exactness in the case of our epic. We have the historical nucleus so to speak in a nutshell in a passage of Eginhard's "Life of Charlemagne," which reads as follows :

"Charles attacked Spain with the greatest possible display of warlike preparation and, having crossed the Pyrenees at a bound and reduced to surrender every castle and town he approached, was returning with his army safe and sound, but that he was fated to experience for a short while the perfidy of the Vascons (Basques) in the pass of that same Pyrenean ridge. For as the army was proceeding directly on its way in a long line, such as the narrowness of the pass allowed of, the Vascons rushed upon the extreme rear, encumbered with the army baggage, out of an ambush disposed on the highest summit, hurled them down into the valley below, and having engaged them at close quarters, killed them every one ; after which they plundered the baggage, and dispersed to all quarters with the utmost celerity, under cover of the night. The Vascons had in their favour the lightness of their armour and the nature of the locality, while this same circumstance and the weight of their armour militated against the Franks and placed them utterly at a disadvantage. In this engagement Eggihard, steward of the royal table, Anselm, Count Palatine, *and Roland, Prefect of the Marches of Brittany, perished with many others.*"

Eginhard mentions the fact more briefly in his "Annals," under the year 778, and concludes with this remark : " This disaster obscured to a great extent in the King's heart the successes he had obtained in Spain."

Dry and matter-of-fact as this account is, one can easily see how the fact itself must have deeply impressed the popular mind, while what we may call the "stage setting" offered ample food for the popular fancy to work out into the most picturesque details. Such national disgrace could not be accepted without an exonerating explanation. The blame must fall on some one head—hence the Villain, the Treason. As for the Hero, he was not far to seek: Roland, as it happened, was a familiar and favourite figure in the company of Paladins which surrounded the majestic central figure—the King; many stories of adventure and knightly exploits were attached to his name and that of his friend Oliver: what worthier, more pathetic culmination than such an end?

A fine material for new ballads! The wandering minstrel ("juggler," *jongleur*), was sure of a good supper and warm bed, —aye, and of some bright coins in his pouch too,—in the castle where, in his monotonous singsong, to the accompaniment of his funny little violin, he entertained the baron and his household (live book that he was!) on a long winter evening, in the great hall, with this or that incident of the great tragedy of Roncevaux: now the treason of Ganelon, then the massacre, or the Archbishop's last blessing—Roland's dying blast on the Olifant—the moving death of fair Aude—the great avenging battle of Saragossa—Ganelon's trial by the ordeal of single combat and his punishment, etc. Several of these disjointed ballads (*cantilènes*), if recited successively, arranged themselves into a more or less consecutive story. Then clerks took a hand at them and worked them into one of those semi-poetical, rudely metrical narratives known as the *Chansons de Geste* (epic lays), until there came one, more learned, equipped with literary training and gifted with a true poet's soul, who, out of the scattered "material," made an epic poem — our "Chanson de Roland."

JUGGLER (JONGLEUR).
(From a MS. in the National Library in Paris, XIth Century.)

Eminent men were more humble-minded in those days, a humility which, moreover, was fostered by the teachings and life of the Christian cloister, the only literary workshop for ages. So they cared more for leaving a fine piece of work than for attaching their name to it. On the other hand, the general public cared for the work and not at all for the worker. Hence we have the works—the "Nibelungenlied," the "Beowulf," the "Chanson de Roland"—but know nothing of any authors.

Neither are the dates of these and similar works given, but have to be approximated from internal evidence. In the case of our *Chanson* the difficulty is less great, owing to two very reliable clews: first, the armours described are those of the eleventh century; and second, Jerusalem is mentioned as being in the power of the Moslems, with no reference to the first crusade, which took place in 1098. *Ergo* —the epic took its final form some time during the eleventh century.

In a Norman-French metrical description

of the Battle of Hastings (1066), it is recorded that Taillefer, William the Conqueror's favourite minstrel (*trouvère*), rode in front of the Norman ranks, singing of Roland at Roncevaux. But it is impossible to decide whether he sang fragments of our *Chanson*, or of the older and ruder *Chanson de Geste*.

THE END

PRONUNCIATION OF UNFAMILIAR NAMES.

(AFTER THE KEY OF THE WEBSTER DICTIONARY.)

Aegir	Ā'-gĭr.
Aix	Āx.
Angantyr	Ăn'-găn-tĭr.
Angurwadel	Ăn"-gŭr-vä'-del.
Atle	Ăt'-lê.
Aude	Aud.
Balder	Băl'-der.
Baligant	Bä'-lig-ànt,
Bele	Bê'-lê.
Björn	Byûrn (*û* as in *but*).
Blancandrin	Blan'-can-drin.
Bramimonda	Brà-mĭ-mon'-dà.
Chanson	Shan(g)-son(g)' (nasal, but do not sound the *g*).
Charlemagne	Shàr-le-màn'-y(e)
Durendal	Dụ-ran(g)-dàl'.
Elli-de	El-lĭ'-dê.
Emir	Ā-meer'.

Esaias	Ē-sá′-yas.
Fafner	Fàf′-ner.
Framnäs	Fràm′-näse.
Frey	Frĕy (the y sounded as in *boy*).
Freya	Frê′-yạ′.
Frithjof	Frit′-iof.
Ganelon	Gà-ne-lon′(g).
Gautier	Gŏ-tyā′.
Halfdan	Hàlf′-dàn.
Halwar	Hàl′-vär.
Ham	Hàm.
Heid	Hĕĭd.
Helge	Hel′-ḡê.
Hilding	Hild′-ing.
Ingeborg	In′-ḡe-borg.
Jumala	Yụ′-mà-là.
Marsilius	Mar-sĭ′-lius.
Naimes	Nāme.
Odin	Ŏ′-din.
Oehlenschläger	Û-len-shlā′-ger.
Oriflamme	Ŏ-rĭ-flàm′.
Pinabel	Pĭ-nà-bel′.
Ring	Ring.
Roncevaux	Ron(g)-se-vŏ′.
Saragossa	Sà-rá-gos′-sà.
Sigurd	Sĭ′-gụrd.
Sote	Sŏ′-tĕ.
Surtur	Sụr′-tụr.
Tegner	Ten′-yer.

Thierri	Tyer-ree'.
Thorsten	Thor'-sten.
Valhalla	Văl-hăl'-lă.
Valkyrie	Văl-kï'-rĭe.
Veillantif	Vê-lyan(g)-tif'.
Vikingson	Vī'-king-son.

Tales of the Heroic Ages.

By ZENAÏDE A. RAGOZIN, author of "Chaldea," "Vedic India," etc.
No. I.—Comprising "Siegfried, the Hero of the North," and "Beowulf, the Hero of the Anglo-Saxons."
Illustrated by Geo. T. Tobin. 12°. $1.50
No. II.—Comprising "Frithjof, the Viking of Norway," and "Roland, the Paladin of France."
Illustrated. 12°. $1.50

"The author is one who knows her subject as a scholar, and has the skill and imagination to construct her stories admirably. Her style is terse and vivid, well adapted to interest the young in these dignified and thrilling tales."—*Dial.*

Plutarch for Boys and Girls.

Selected and Edited by JOHN S. WHITE. Illustrated. 8°. $1.75
Library edition. 2 vols. 16° 2.50

"It is a pleasure to see in so beautiful and elegant a form one of the great books of the world. The best Plutarch for young readers."—*Literary World.*

"Shows admirable scholarship and judgment."—*Critic.*

Pliny for Boys and Girls.

The Natural History of Pliny the Elder. Edited for Boys and Girls by JOHN S. WHITE. With 52 illustrations. 4° . $2.00

"Mr. White's selections are admirably made. He has gleaned in all directions for his notes; and the result is one which reflects on him great credit, and adds another to the number of juvenile books which may be commended without reservation."—*Independent.*

"For the libraries of the young—and every boy and girl in the land should collect a library of their own—these superb books have a special adaptation; they open the classics to them."—*Boston Journal of Education.*

Herodotus for Boys and Girls.

Edited by JOHN S. WHITE. With 50 illustrations. 8° . $1.75
Library edition. 2 vols. 16° 2.50

"The book really contains those parts of Herodotus which a judicious parent would most likely have his boys and girls acquainted with, and Mr. White has succeeded in condensing these by omitting multitudes of phrases inserted in the Greek text. The print is so large and clear that no one need fear that it will foster a tendency to near-sightedness on the part of boy or girl."—*Nation.*

The Travels of Marco Polo.

Edited for Boys and Girls, with explanatory notes and comments, by THOMAS W. KNOX. With over 200 illustrations. 8°. $1.75

"To the student of geography Marco Polo needs no introduction. He is revered as the greatest of all travellers in the Middle Ages, and by more than one careful geographer his work is believed to have led to the discovery of the New World by the Hardy Mariner of Genoa. . . . The story of his travels was received with incredulity, and he died while Europe was gravely doubting its truth. It has remained for later generations to establish the correctness of his narrative and accord him the praise he so richly deserves."

G. P. PUTNAM'S SONS. NEW YORK AND LONDON

TALES OF HEROISM.

By E. S. Brooks

FOUR VOLUMES; OCTAVO. ILLUSTRATED. EACH $2.00

I. HISTORIC BOYS: Their Endeavors, Their Achievements, and Their Times. With 29 full-page illustrations.

"Told with a spirit that makes them capital reading for boys. Mr. Brooks writes in a clear and vivacious English, and has caught the art of throwing into high relief the salient points of his stories."—*Christian Union.*

II. HISTORIC GIRLS. Stories of Girls Who Have Influenced the History of Their Times. With 20 full-page illustrations.

"The Tales are well written, well and generously illustrated, open avenues for further profitable reading, and are good from cover to cover."—*Chicago Advance.*

III. CHIVALRIC DAYS, and Youthful Deeds. With 51 illustrations.

"The historic episodes upon which these stories are based are well chosen, and handled with considerable skill and picturesqueness."—*N. Y. Evening Mail.*

IV. HEROIC HAPPENINGS, Told in Verse and Story. With 42 illustrations.

"Fortunate indeed will be the boy or girl who has these fascinating pages put into his or her hands."—*Public Opinion*, Washington, D. C.

G. P. PUTNAM'S SONS

NEW YORK
27 WEST 23D STREET

LONDON
24 BEDFORD ST., STRAND

THE RAIL AND WATER SERIES
BY KIRK MUNROE

Fully illustrated, 12mo, each $1 25

I.—Under Orders. The Story of a Young Reporter.

"It is pleasure to open a juvenile book and find in it live people—characters that are neither impossible paragons of goodness nor chimerical examples of success. Such a book is 'Under Orders.' Boys who want to know what a reporter's life is will get a fair idea of it from this very interesting book."
—*Buffalo Courier.*

"No one can tell a better story, or tell it in a more interesting manner. The book is an excellent one for boys."—*Christian at Work.*

II.—Prince Dusty. A Story of the Oil Regions.

"This is the prince of writers for boys. He always has something fresh and interesting to tell them, and reaches their hearts every time. His books are full of adventure, yet free from exaggeration and sensationalism."

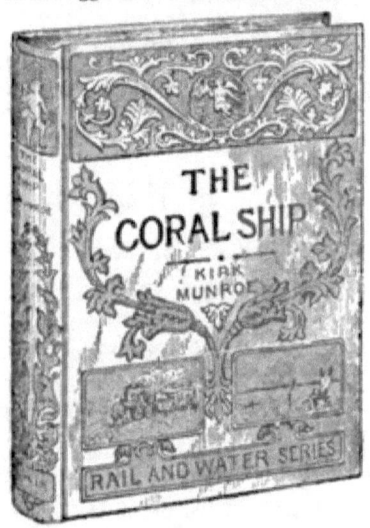

III.—Cab and Caboose. A Story of Railroad Life.

"From the time Rod Blake wins the bicycle race and becomes the proud possessor of the Railroad Cup, all through the narrative, with its thrilling adventures and escapes from wreck, fire, robbers, tramps, and, worse than all, from an attempt to fasten a crime upon him, the boy readers (and surely girls too) will not find a dull page."

IV.—The Coral Ship. A Story of the Florida Reef.

"No one need have any hesitancy in regard to buying a book by Mr. Kirk Munroe, who has been justly styled 'the prince of writers of books for boys,' for he has the happiest possible faculty of being able to interest young people. He knows what they like to be told, and his books have a decided charm. The adventures narrated, while exciting, are real, and are not calculated to produce any unhealthy effect upon their readers."

G. P. PUTNAM'S SONS, NEW YORK AND LONDON

FAIRY TALES OF THE NATIONS

English Fairy Tales.
Collected by Joseph Jacobs, President of the English Folk-Lore Society. Pictured by John D. Batten. 12mo . . . $1 75
New and cheaper edition 1 25

Celtic Fairy Tales.
Collected by Joseph Jacobs. Pictured by John D. Batten. Uniform with above. 12mo $1 75
New and cheaper edition 1 25

Indian Fairy Tales.
Collected and edited by Joseph Jacobs. Pictured by John D. Batten. 12mo. $1 75

More English Fairy Tales: Comprising the second selection of the successful series of "English Fairy Tales." Compiled by Joseph Jacobs, and illustrated by J. D. Batten. Uniform with "English Fairy Tales." Square 8vo $1 75
New and cheaper edition 1 25

More Celtic Fairy Tales: Comprising the second selection of the successful "Celtic Fairy Tales." Compiled by Joseph Jacobs, and illustrated by J. D. Batten. 12mo $1 75
New and cheaper edition 1 25

"Mr. Jacobs relates their marvels racily and in a way to hold the ear of either a child or a student of this fascinating branch of folk-lore."—*Christian Union.*

"Mr. Jacobs' works are always entertaining and valuable, and his series of fairy books grows in interest with each new volume."—*New York Post.*

Chinese Nights Entertainments.
Forty Tales Related by Almond-Eyed Folk. Actors in the Romance of "The Strayed Arrow." By Adele M. Fielde. With illustrations by Chinese artists. Uniform with above volumes. 12mo.
$1 75

The Cruikshank Fairy Book.
Four Famous Stories. I. Puss in Boots. II. Jack and the Bean-Stalk. III. Hop-o'-My-Thumb. IV. Cinderella. With 40 reproductions of the characteristic designs of George Cruikshank. Large 8vo, full gilt edges, handsomely stamped cover . . . $2 00

G. P. PUTNAM'S SONS, NEW YORK AND LONDON.

www.ingramcontent.com/pod-product-compliance
Lightning Source LLC
Chambersburg PA
CBHW030318240426
43673CB00040B/1205